Tamaki-makaurau

Myths and legends
of Auckland Landmarks

Edith Phillips-Gibson
August 2006.

Edith Phillips-Gibson
Illustrations by Loc Keokatavong

REED

REED PUBLISHING (NZ) LTD
TE KARUHI TĀ TĀPUI O REED (AOTEAROA)
Established in 1907, Reed is New Zealand's largest
book publisher, with over 600 titles in print.
www.reed.co.nz

Published by Reed Books, a division of Reed Publishing (NZ) Ltd, 39 Rawene Road, Birkenhead,
Auckland 10. Associated companies, branches and representatives throughout the world.

© 2006 Edith Phillips-Gibson — text and maps
© 2006 Loc Keokatavong — illustrations
The authors assert their moral rights in the work.

A catalogue entry for this book is available from the
National Library of New Zealand.

ISBN 10: 0 7900 1061 5
ISBN 13: 978 0 7900 1061 8
First published 2006
Designed by Debbie Talbot-King
Printed in China

Contents

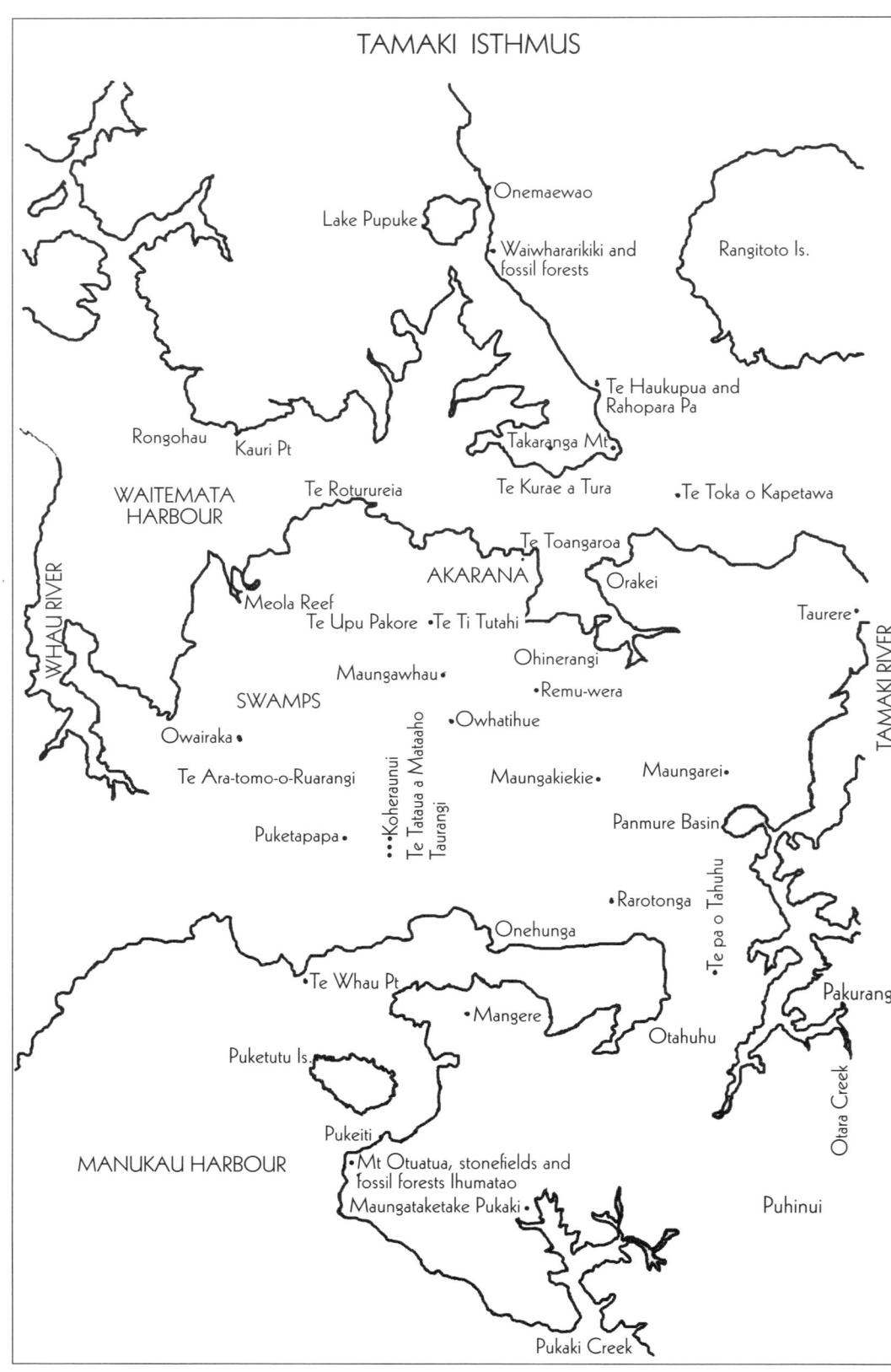

TAMAKI ISTHMUS

Onemaewao

Lake Pupuke

Waiwhararikiki and fossil forests

Rangitoto Is.

Te Haukupua and Rahopara Pa

Rongohau

Kauri Pt

Takaranga Mt

WAITEMATA HARBOUR

Te Roturureia

Te Kurae a Tura

Te Toka o Kapetawa

WHAU RIVER

Te Toangaroa

AKARANA

Orakei

Taurere

Meola Reef

Te Upu Pakore

Te Ti Tutahi

TAMAKI RIVER

Ohinerangi

Maungawhau

Remu-wera

SWAMPS

Owhatihue

Owairaka

Te Ara-tomo-o-Ruarangi

Koheraunui
Te Tataua a Mataaho
Taurangi

Maungakiekie

Maungarei

Puketapapa

Panmure Basin

Rarotonga

Te pa o Tahuhu

Onehunga

Te Whau Pt

Pakurang

Mangere

Otahuhu

Puketutu Is.

Otara Creek

Pukeiti

MANUKAU HARBOUR

Mt Otuatua, stonefields and fossil forests Ihumatao

Maungataketake Pukaki

Puhinui

Pukaki Creek

Introduction

The isthmus of Tamaki is the narrow passageway that links the Waikato and southern North Island to Northland. The four seas on the eastern side of the isthmus were known to Maori as the four seas of Tamaki: Maraetai, Ti Kapa, Waitemata and Te Rapu Mauana. These were formed from drowned river valleys, which became the harbours.

Many thousands of men, women and children lived on the isthmus, but times could be tough. Research has shown that most of the Maori people lived an average of only 40 years. Their clothing was not ideal for the climate and they mostly went barefoot. Conditions in the whare were very basic and uncomfortable, food was sometimes scarce, and like all races they got sick. Even with the tohunga's karakia they were only able to cure a few illnesses. Herbal cures were not much used before the arrival of Europeans, although Maori were very good at healing the wounds inflicted during battles.

The tribes who lived on top of some of the area's 48 volcanoes needed strong defences for their pa. Anyone travelling through this area had to pass through the narrow isthmus of Tamaki, and sometimes there were conflicts. Whenever they were threatened the people who lived here would gather plenty of food, firewood and water, then retreat to the safety of their pa, where they could be besieged for months. The many volcanoes on the Tamaki isthmus were ideal for building pa on, and made great lookouts. The way the volcanoes formed also meant that they nearly all had large caves in them. Today some of these are regarded as dangerous, and they have been blocked off.

Most battles were fought in summer after the kumara had been planted. Before going into battle the warriors would chant powerful karakia. Usually the warriors were naked during the battle; clothes took a long time to make, so it was not the custom to damage them during a fight. When the Maori people fought they rarely killed each other because their weapons — taiaha, tewhatewha and mere — were not very sharp. Most of the time the plan was simply to terrify the enemy, and often a battle was over when the first warrior was killed. The rest of the taua would run away, chased by the conquering tribe, who would take as slaves anyone they caught. Records that claim thousands were killed in one battle were probably exaggerated, and it is likely that diseases killed more people than warfare.

The other inhabitants of the Tamaki isthmus were the patupaiarehe, the fairy people, or 'children of the mist'. They had fair skins, and they could not eat the food of this world. If they did they would die. It is thought that the Maori people, on their many journeys around the Pacific Ocean, must have had some contact with the European or pale-skinned people long before recorded history, which was the origin of these 'children of the mist'.

Many of the names associated with places on the Tamaki isthmus relate to people who lived there, and they often record events that happened in their lives. Wairaka of Owairaka (Mt Albert) is an ancient equivalent of today's liberated woman. Ruarangi was a large chief from the same area. On one occasion his tribe escaped their pursuers by travelling through a cave on the mountainside, but because he was so big Ruarangi was unable to squeeze through a narrow opening inside the cave and follow them to freedom. To this day the cave is known as Te-Ara-Tomo-o-Ruarangi.

Some say that Ruarangi and his people dug this cave. In geological terms the cave, like all the others in the Tamaki area, is a lava 'tube', created as lava cooled on its outer surface and the hot lava inside drained away. Most of the caves on Auckland's volcanoes were recorded by the late Les Kermode of the Auckland Geology Club.

It is not possible to describe all the pa sites that are mentioned in this book, but some are integral to the stories. Owairaka is one of these. It is thought that at one time it was home to as many as 1570 people. To defend its circumference 45 people were needed every 20 metres. The pa was heavily fortified by terracing, ditching, palisades and stone walls. Over the years, wars, epidemics and the arrival of the Europeans took their toll, drastically reducing the population. In 1820, when Samuel Marsden climbed Owairaka with the chief Apihau Kawau, it was deserted. Today no evidence of the pa remains because in 1867 the mountain was quarried for supplies of scoria to build railways. Although it was declared a reserve in 1880 the removal of the scoria continued until 1929. This has happened to other Tamaki volcanoes too, although all are now protected. In size, Rangitoto is by far the largest volcano. Millions of years ago the Waitakeres were the highest volcanoes in Tamaki, but over time they have worn down, and Maungawhau (Mt Eden) is now the highest. Most of what is left of the Waikakere volcanoes are the hard rock plugs of the volcanoes' craters. A good example of this is Lion Rock, at Piha.

Maungakiekie was the most extensively fortified pa of them all. It had three levels of palisades. The top section, the tihi, was the strongest point. If all else failed the tribe could grab all the food and water they needed and retreat to the mountaintop. To the southwest of the tihi there are burial caverns. The tangata whenua buried a huge number of people here, lowering their bodies into the caverns. These are called Te Tupootetini (the burial caverns or pits of the many).

As far as possible, the stories and myths of Tamaki are retold here as they might have been in earlier times. Some of the stories have been passed down through many generations, and there can be several different versions of the same story. Sometimes the story varies according to who is telling it. The stories of some areas are hard to find, while others are better known. For example, stories about Maniopoto, whose daughters-in-law lived in the Maungakiekie pa, are easy to find. These stories have been sourced mainly from George Graham's manuscripts (kept at the Auckland Museum library archive) and from historical records kept by councils. It is difficult to pinpoint some of the places mentioned, some of which will be mythical. A special thanks to David Simmons, who was able to clarify some missing data.

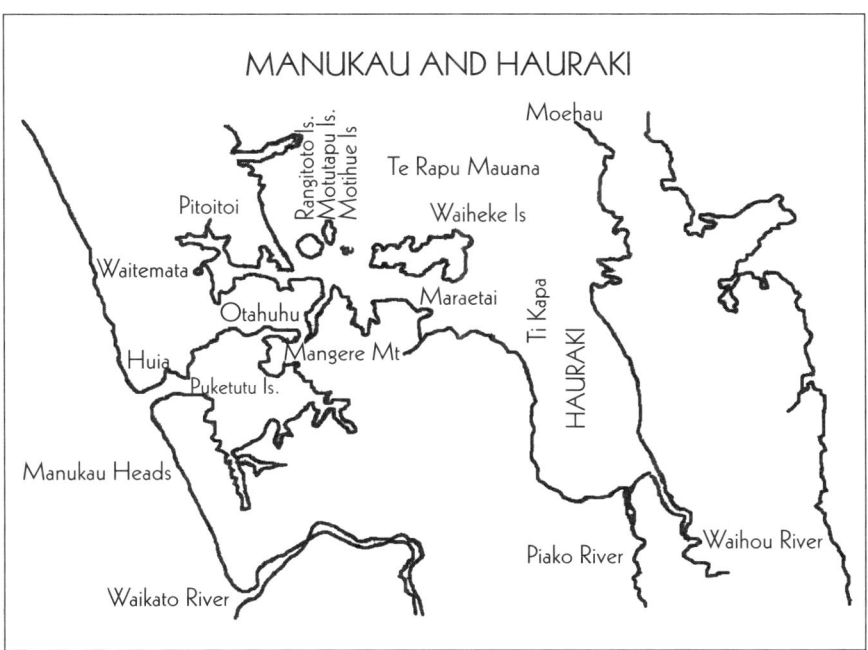

Taniwha

It is believed that the Maori had historical memories of encounters with crocodiles in other Pacific countries, and taniwha often feature in their stories. Sometimes taniwha are portrayed in a violent manner, but some of them have a more kindly nature. Ureia and Haumia (see 'Ureia the Taniwha', page 16) were actually thought to be pet seals or whales and not taniwha at all.

The taniwha Pane Irairi accompanied the Tainui canoe in the Manukau Harbour, guiding the canoe by travelling in front of it. Pane had freckles on his head and an arched back, and he swam on the surface of the ocean. At Otara Pane tried to swim up the creek, but it was too shallow and he had to retreat, so he stayed in the area after that.

Paikea was a Northland taniwha who often visited his friends at Anawhata. While in the area he ate the flotsam and jetsam that floated by. Paikea would help the people by carrying them across the entrance to the Manukau Harbour and back.

Mokoika-hiku-waru was a taniwha with eight lizard-like tails, who lived in a deep pool in the Tamaki River. To make it more comfortable he dug the pool even deeper. Nearby was the Panmure Lagoon where he got nearly all the food he wanted. The people called it 'Te kai o Mokoika'. This lagoon provided food exclusively for Mokoika for many years, and it is only recently that fish have been caught there.

When the *Arawa* canoe came one of the chiefs brought two lizards, who were known as Nga Ngarara a Kahu. When the canoe stopped at Oruawharu the chief placed one lizard on Rangitoto and one on Motutapu. These lizards became taniwha and eventually turned into stone.

Mangere

Lazy Winds

The mountain called Te Upoko o Mataaho (the head of Mataaho) erupted 18,000 years ago. Mataaho, the giant god of volcanoes, was responsible for this eruption, and he left his footprints nearby, to the south of Mangere at Pukaki. This area is called Nga Tapuwaeamataaho (the footprints of Mataaho).

When Hotoroa, a chief on the Tainui canoe, visited the mountain he felt gentle breezes blowing and told Taiheku, who named the mountain Nga Hau Mangere.

The Dogskin Path

Some of the Tainui people settled at Nga Hau Mangere and built a small pa there. Later, Ngati Whatua attacked and conquered the group, but Tainui descendants returned to the pa. In time the Waiohua had control of the pa, but there were not enough people to defend it properly, so they spread seashells all around it.

They thought that the scrunch of the shells would warn them that someone was coming, but unfortunately this didn't protect them.

After Tahataha of the Waiohua murdered his sister, Tuperiri sought utu. Tuperiri led the taua of Te Taou from Ngati Whatua in what was called 'the battle of the warriors'. So that their approach to the pa would not be heard, they laid their dogskin cloaks down on the shells. The taua then crept carefully across these and easily defeated the small tribe.

Afterwards this became known as the battle of Te Aratopuni (the dogskin path). Only a few of the Mangere people escaped, and some of them hid in a lava cave nearby. When the Ngati Whatua found them they built a huge fire at the entrance to the cave and lit it. When the fire died down they went inside and cut up the cooked bodies, then they feasted on them.

Much later some of the Waiohua returned, seeking safety here from Ngati Whatua after Kiwi Tamaki was killed at Paruroa (see 'Kiwi Tamaki', page 25).

Near Mangere there are two buried forests known as the Ihumatao fossil forests. One of these was buried in a peat swamp 100,000 years ago, and was waterlogged for thousands of years. Now erosion has exposed this fossil forest on the beach, and the preserved trunks of the kauri trees can be seen and walked on. The other forest was buried 30,000 years ago in ash showers from Maungataketake volcano. Parts of this forest can be seen on the cliffs, otherwise it needs to be dug up.

Manukau Heads

Muriwai

Erangi Pt

Te Henga

Anawhata

Piha

WAITAKERE

Karekare

Te Ahauahu Pt

Marotiri

Manukau Heads

Whatipu

Karanga a Hape

Puponga Pt

Titirangi

Puketutu Is.

Onehunga

Waitemata Harbour

Akarana

Manukau Harbour

Awhitu

Tasman Sea

Ureia the Taniwha

About the end of the seventeenth century the Hauraki people had a pet taniwha called Ureia. They regarded Ureia not as a taniwha but as a guardian tipua. She was their mauri. When a disaster was about to happen Ureia would become alert. She would come out of her rua in Te Kirikiri River and rise up so that the enemy could see her. If the people at her pa were overrun and many killed, she would swim out to sea. There she would roll her body from side to side in the surf, sending columns of spray high into the air.

Ureia had an enormous appetite. One day the taniwha Haumia, who was the tipua of the Waikato tribe, invited Ureia to visit, to feast on the lush grasses that grew at Manukau. Ureia was reluctant to accept because she did not trust Haumia. He was able to talk through the tohunga of his tribe, and he advised his people to kill Ureia when she came to visit.

Haumia went to Te Kirikiri to see Ureia, and promised her that she would receive many presents if she agreed to visit — huia and kotuku, raukawa trees, speargrass, kopura, manehau and kohuhu trees. Ureia was still reluctant to leave her home, so Haumia chanted the spells that his tohunga had woven to weaken her willpower. This made Ureia agree to come after all.

The taniwha swam up the Hauraki Gulf to Te Rerenga-wairua and down the west coast to the Manukau. On the way Ureia stopped to scratch her back on the rocks at a place that came to be called Te Roturuoureia (the comb of Ureia).

Inside the Manukau Harbour at Puponga, Haumia's tribe had constructed a monstrous net in the shape of a house, made of the strongest ropes, and had assembled 1000 men on each side of the net. As Ureia approached the harbour her tail was stranded on a sandbank, which to her was an omen foretelling her death. Meanwhile Haumia's tohunga stood on Puketutu Island chanting spells. Haumia swam safely over the trap, then the tohunga signalled the men on either side of it. When Ureia reached Puponga she was trapped. When the chief Hape saw that Ureia had been captured he called out loudly, 'We've got her!'

Ureia was immensely strong, and in her attempts to escape she writhed and struggled as the tide went out four times and came flooding back in three times. Never had anyone known a taniwha to have such strength and endurance. Ureia really tested the lasting power of those holding the ropes.

During this amazing battle for survival Ureia threw up huge sandhills and filled the mouth of the Manukau Harbour with the sand. But finally the Waikato people got the better of Ureia and killed her. They cut her into pieces, cooked her and ate her.

Since the killing of Ureia it has been dangerous to cross the bar at Manukau Heads. This has to be done carefully and only at high tide. Many unwary sailors have drowned and boats have sunk since that time.

Kaiwhare, 'The House Eater'

The taniwha Kaiwhare had a lair at Te Rua o Kaiwhare at Piha. He also had lairs at Manukau Heads, Awhitu, Whatipu and Te Henga. Kaiwhare was famous for making flood tides and flipping canoes over to drown the people in them, who he would then eat.

Paikea, a guardian spirit, lived in the same area, and when people got into difficulty at sea Paikea would help them to reach safety.

To keep Kaiwhare happy the people made little houses on rafts. Into these they would put food for the taniwha, and when the tide started to go out they would set the rafts adrift. If they could not see the rafts the next morning then they felt it was safe to go fishing. Kaiwhare got his name because it means 'house eater', but he had a preference for eating people.

During quiet evenings Kaiwhare would lie motionless below the gently surging water just outside the harbour bar, waiting to spot the glow from the torches of fishermen wading in the shallow water to spear flounder. Then, without any warning, Kaiwhare would swim swiftly over the bar and snatch a tasty meal of man, woman or child. Soon the fishermen no longer dared to venture near the heads of the harbour.

The people were very dependent on this rich fishing ground for food, and it was not long before the tribe began to starve. Something had to be done to get rid of Kaiwhare. But no one was brave enough to face the terrible scaly taniwha. They had seen his bulging eyes searching for them and his long, twisting tail flicking in and out of the thundering white surf. They decided to seek help.

At Hauraki, on the other side of the North Island, lived a strong man named Tamure. He possessed a mere pounamu which was so powerful that a single blow with it would kill a taniwha. Tamure was in fact a powerful giant who travelled by striding from hilltop to hilltop.

A messenger was sent to ask Tamure for his help. He agreed to come, and a few steps brought him to Awhitu, on the southern shore of the Manukau Harbour, where many people waited for him.

'I shall deal with Kaiwhare,' Tamure said in his booming, fearless voice. He didn't even need the help of the people at Maraetai, who had offered their assistance because they were relatives of the Manukau tribe.

The next day Tamure went to the headland above Kaiwhare's lair. When night came, the fishermen went down to the beach with their flaming torches and pronged spears. Tamure also sent the men out in their canoes to lure Kaiwhare out of his cave. As the sun slowly sank into the sea, Kaiwhare smelled 'man meat'. He licked his sharp teeth and emerged rumbling from the seabed. His strong tail knocked rocks aside and waves dashed upon the shore as his monstrous head rose threateningly above the water. Tamure, wise in the ways of taniwha slaying, brought his mere pounamu crashing down, shattering the taniwha's massive skull. Then, in a few strides, Tamure was gone.

Kaiwhare thrashed in agony. His huge tail swept rocks and steep cliffs into the sea, leaving an area of smooth rock behind. Waves pounded the cliffs in tall pillars of foam and water. Kaiwhare was strong, but the deadly mere of Tamure had wounded him so badly that he was never able to cross the bar again. From that time on the taniwha has had to be satisfied with a diet of crayfish and octopus.

To this day one of Tamure's large footprints can be seen on the sand dune at Maioro. The footprint has never been covered by sand and a spring flows from this spot. Also deep in the sand are moa bones — perhaps Kaiwhare ate these too.

The Lovers

Two kilometres from Huia in the Karamatua Valley lived a Waiohua woman. One summer she fell in love with a young Kawerau warrior whose tribe were camped there to fish. There were plentiful fish to be caught and many succulent shellfish. Huia was a favourite place for the Kawerau, and they had a heavily fortified pa above Huia at Te Komoki.

The people of the young woman's tribe were not happy, and they told her she had to leave her lover and return to her home without him. The young lovers desperately wanted to stay together so they hid under a waterfall. It took several days for the tribe to find them, and by then the constant drumming of the falling water had made them temporarily deaf. It was several days before they could hear again. The waterfall where they were found was then named Kainga-maturi (the dwelling place of the deaf).

Awhitu

In about 1740 an important battle took place. Ngati Whatua set out to secure the Whatipu area before they attacked the stronger forts of the Waiohua at Mangawhau and Maungakiekie. They sent the chief Te Taou with a taua to attack two of the pa there. When they arrived, however, they discovered that the canoes they expected were not at the northern headland.

But this did not discourage them. They set about making rafts of flax stalks and driftwood. Then they crossed the channel during the night and surprised the people at Awhitu and Tarataua. Most of the hapu at these pa were killed. Further on, at Pukehorokatoa, the war party was repelled, but they had succeeded in what they set out to do and left to take part in the battles at Maungawhau and Maungakiekie.

Maungakiekie

The Mountain of War

Some 20,000 years ago, after the extinction of the dinosaurs and before the arrival of man, Maungakiekie erupted from the ground through three craters. Streams of molten lava spilled over the cones, building them higher and higher.

There was once a large bay nearby, but as Maungakiekie grew this was completely filled. So violently did the volcano blow that the seawater was thrust back, making a long tidal wave out into the South Pacific Ocean. Above, the mountain became taller and taller as it spouted ash and rocks over the surrounding countryside. Maungakiekie is a 'shield' mountain, with gently sloping sides and a high buttress of basalt rock at the top. Beneath the volcano many moa were buried, and those that survived made homes in the lava caves on the mountain.

At the time of the Great Fleet, about AD 1400, the people of the *Tainui* canoe settled on the isthmus. They found other people inhabiting the area, and after many years and many marriages to Nga Oho, Ngaiwi and Ngati-tai, the tribe came to be known as the Waiohua.

The people living here needed protection, and they skilfully set about building the pa on Maungakiekie. This took a long time and a lot of energy. Making the terraces on the rocky mountain was difficult. The soil was easy to dig, but the koto maori was not as wide as a modern spade. Many of the rocks were extremely heavy, so many men were needed to move them. These rocks were pushed into hollows to fill them up, then soil was carried up in baskets and tipped on top of the rocks. This created the flat areas, where beautifully carved whare and food platforms were built. At first the pa was called Nga Whakairo a Titahi. Titahi had the terraces dug out in such a way that they showed the same patterns as he had on his tattoo. He and his tribe, Ngati Awa, also had a pa and village at Owairaka.

One day word came that Ngati Whatua were approaching. Fearing that they intended to wage war, the Waiohua and their slaves set about further strengthening the defences at all their hill pa. Extensive earthworks and palisades were built at Maungakiekie, making it the best Maori fortification in the land. Any attacking force now needed to defeat three levels of defences. Each time they would be showered with heavy rocks, and they would also have to win the hand-to-hand fighting with the taiaha and the mere.

Wars were so frequent that soon all the Waitemata tribes joined forces with the Waiohua to form one large tribal group.

Kiwi Tamaki

One day Te Tahuri and the chief Ikamaupoho had a baby boy, who was named Kiwi Tamaki. Just after Kiwi was born, powerful karakia were chanted. At some time in his life Kiwi moved to Maungakiekie. As he grew he learned to be skilful in the ways of war, and in about 1720 he became chief of the Waiohua. But Kiwi was really a wicked bandit — had he not been the chief he would have been a hunted criminal. His tribe was the most powerful in the land and could have lived in peace, yet under Kiwi's rule they were frequently at war. They won almost all their battles, and attempts by many tribes to defeat the Waiohua at the Maungakiekie pa failed. It was their stronghold.

Kiwi Tamaki would call his warriors to meetings, or warn them of danger, by beating his great greenstone-decorated pahu. The pahu made a fairly high-pitched note, and this resounded from the top of Maungakiekie, close to the sacred totara tree that grew there. He also used a pukaea, which meant the gong could be heard for kilometres across the countryside.

Although Kiwi Tamaki was a cruel and relentless warrior, he could be very welcoming to friendly tribes. He would arrange huge hui, with wonderful songs and entertainment. The tribe would collect vast quantities of food from the surrounding areas, and Kiwi's mother, Te Tahuri, would expertly supervise the cooking.

The Waiohua had an enormous fleet of canoes on both harbours so that they could fish and travel whenever they wished. Kiwi Tamaki became the most famous chief of the isthmus.

Kiwi was very sure of his strength and power, and at times he was reckless when he should have been more careful. At one time Ngati Whatua did battle with the outlying members of the Waiohua and gained possession of the Kaipara area. When the chief Tumu-paki died, Kiwi was invited to an uhanga (a mourning ceremony) at Waituoro. When he and his followers arrived they had weapons hidden under their clothes, and during the night they cruelly murdered some of the entertainers while they slept. Kiwi also killed the chief Tupeiri's sister and another chieftainess. He claimed this wicked act was utu for the defeat Ngati Whatua had inflicted on the Waiohua at Kaipara several years earlier.

A hasty Ngati Whatua taua formed and set off in pursuit as Kiwi and his party hurried off in the darkness. At Titirangi, after some fierce fighting, Kiwi was defeated and he then retreated back to Maungakiekie. A powerful army of warriors set off after him, some of them coming by canoe from Pitoitoi. This army destroyed all of Kiwi's villages on the shores of the Waitemata, except Te Matarae.

Near Little Muddy Creek, at the 'Battle of Paruroa', Kiwi's warriors approached the shore where the Ngati Whatua taua were camped. Rather than defending himself at Maungakiekie, Kiwi foolishly chose to fight on open ground. The Ngati Whatua chief Waha-akiaki ordered his taua to perform

'hawaike-pepeke'. They pretended to retreat up a hill. Kiwi's warriors followed. When they reached the ridge of the hill Te Waha-akiaki put a calabash of oil on the ground. This was the signal to turn and attack the Waiohua.

Kiwi tried to escape by canoe but Te Waha-akiaki recognised him by the huia feathers on his head. Te Waha-akiaki leapt out into the water and into the canoe. Both warriors fell onto the beach, and before Kiwi Tamaki could rise the Ngati Whatua chief raised his mere and brought it crashing down on his head.

After Kiwi Tamaki's death the tribe lost the will to fight. It is recorded that in the fight at Paruroa about 3000 of Kiwi's warriors were killed. The corpses were left to rot on the beach, where they polluted the shellfish and made the area tapu for a long time. Those who survived retreated to Maungakiekie.

After his death Kiwi's body was cut up, and the god Rehua was found inside him. One of the Te Taou ate Rehua, and promptly died. Kiwi's body was then hung from a puriri tree at Tauwhare.

After resting and feasting, the Ngati Whatua warriors fought a strongly defended battle and won possession of the pa at Maungakiekie. Chief Tuperiri's people enlarged the terraces at the pa to create an area for more family living and storehouses. This they called Hikurangi. Eventually, around 1780, the Ngati Whatua tribes took all the Waitakere pa from the Waiohua and gained control of the whole isthmus. Te Tuperiri ruled the now abandoned country area from Maungakiekie. Ngati Whatua had also lost many of their tribe, so they were unable to engage in any further fighting. They lived on at the pa but avoided all conflict. Ngati Whatua men married the attractive Waiohua women who were captured, and this gave them full claim to all the Waiohua territory. Other tribal groups moved into the undefended isthmus and settled, building homes and planting gardens.

> Kiwi Tamaki vowed to hang Te Waha-akiaki's breastbone from the sacred totara tree on Maungakiekie.

Patupaiarehe Maungakiekie

In the days of the patupaiarehe (the fairy people), which was so long ago that no one knows how many thousands of years it was, the Waiohua tribe claimed that the patupaiarehe lived in the dense, dark bush at Hunua and Waitakere. Some claim that these people are still there.

On the Tamaki isthmus there was a flat area near Maungawhau with low hills and lakes, and it was here that the patupaiarehe hunted birds. Tamaireia and Hinemairangi were two fairy people who met in this area when they came with their slaves to hunt. Tamaireia liked Hinemairangi so much that he persuaded her to run away with him to Hikurangi.

Hinemairangi's family were very upset that she had fallen in love with a man who they thought was not good enough for her. Besides, this young man lived out west. Rangitira Koiwi-riki gathered a taua together and they set off to Hikurangi to win back their precious kahurangi (jewel).

They caught up with Tamaireia's party at Pakuranga, and here the Hunua tohunga made the sun rise early. As a result they were able to attack and kill many of the Waitakere warriors. The following night the Waitakere fairies heard them coming and were ready to defend themselves. They used a line of tohunga who chanted powerful karakia to turn the Hunua fairies away, but it didn't work. They kept coming. The tohunga raised their voices with even stronger karakia. The ground trembled and the trees shook but still the Hunua fairies kept coming. Angrily the tohunga shouted their strongest karakia.

The ground rocked violently and bulged upwards. The trees fell flat on their sides. A huge split appeared in the ground and fire gushed high into the air. The explosion continued, spilling fire over the Hunua war party. When all were destroyed, Mount Maungakiekie stood on the land where the battle had been fought. Those who escaped had to return to Hunua.

The Waitakere tohunga now had to perform one more powerful incantation, as the wind had changed and was blowing volcanic sparks towards their precious forests. This karakia caused a deluge of rain to occur, and the fires were extinguished. After this Hinemairangi, Tamaireia and the tohunga returned to live happily at Waitakere. But this last karakia was not undone, and Waitakere still gets more rain than anywhere else in Tamaki.

Te Totara i Ahua

A tapu totara once grew on One Tree Hill. It had been there for centuries, growing from the stick of totara that had been used to cut the umbilical cord of the newborn Korokino, who was an ariki child. His father was the chief Tupaha and his mother Hine-te-ao. A tohunga chanted beautiful karakia for the ancient rite of tohi.

It was unusual for a stick of totara to be used to cut the cord, because usually a club was used. It meant that Korokino showed his dedication to Tane, god of the forest, rather than to Tu, the god of war. The cutting was planted and carefully watered for the first few years of its life.

The tree grew tall and strong, although it was buffeted by gale-force winds many times during its 250 years of life. Then, in about 1853, someone cut the tree down to build a house. Using such a tapu tree for a home was exceptionally unlucky, and the people who lived in it all died shortly afterwards.

It is claimed that one day, when a Pakeha can get another totara to grow on the top of Maungakiekie, we will all become truly tangata whenua, just as the Maori people are today.

Maungakiekie was named after the kiekie plant, which used to grow on the trees on the mountain. When people came to live there the bush was cleared.

Despite the myth about the totara tree, it was actually a large pohutukawa that grew on the mountain. It was reliably identified, and either fell over and rotted or was cut down for firewood. Yet perhaps both trees did exist together for a couple of hundred years.

Maungarei

The Watchful Mountain

Maungarei was known to the Maori as the watchful mountain, or the mountain of Reipae. A Tainui ancestress, Reipae, later travelled on to Northland in the form of a bird.

In the story of Kiwi and Rautao (page 64) this mountain was decisively conquered, but because there are no stories recorded about this very strong pa its history has to be different to the other volcanoes.

Before Rangitoto erupted, Maungarei was the youngest volcano on the isthmus. It is only about 9000 years old. Maungarei's first eruption was inside a ring-like area. Some of the raised land on this ring was destroyed, and a steep-sided cone with two craters built up very quickly. A shower of fine dust covered the surrounding flat land, and some scoria 'bombs' fell on the western side of the Tamaki. Around the Panmure area, rich soil developed which was ideal for gardening.

The last eruption was very destructive. The lava filled the crater and overflowed. As it travelled down the mountain it split into two streams and spread all the way to Te Kopuke. Here it filled the river valley and dammed the water, forming Lake Waiatarua. In the Penrose area the soft pink clay in the riverbed oozed up through the super-hot lava and baked hard. In time the water from the river seeped into the ground and came up as a spring at Waipuna. This water filled the basin, creating a small lake. Much later the water burst a bank and flowed out, taking the pumice sand with it and spreading it over much of the Tamaki valley. This, or volcanic activity, changed the course of the Waikato River; previously it had flowed into the Manukau, but now it flowed out at Port Waikato. This is the real reason the Manukau Heads now has the sandbar. There is no longer enough water flowing out of the harbour to wash the sand away. As the Waikato River was still close by, a portage was used to travel to it.

The Maungarei pa had stone walls of brown scoria around the base of the mountain. Inside this were large huts and food platforms. On the terraced slopes high palisades (maioro) were erected; these were made of tree trunks laced together with vines. Behind the palisades were platforms for the warriors to stand on when they were defending the pa. The narrow gateways were easy to defend, but if a battle was not going well these platforms enabled the defenders to retreat step by step to the top. Enemy taua, however, had very

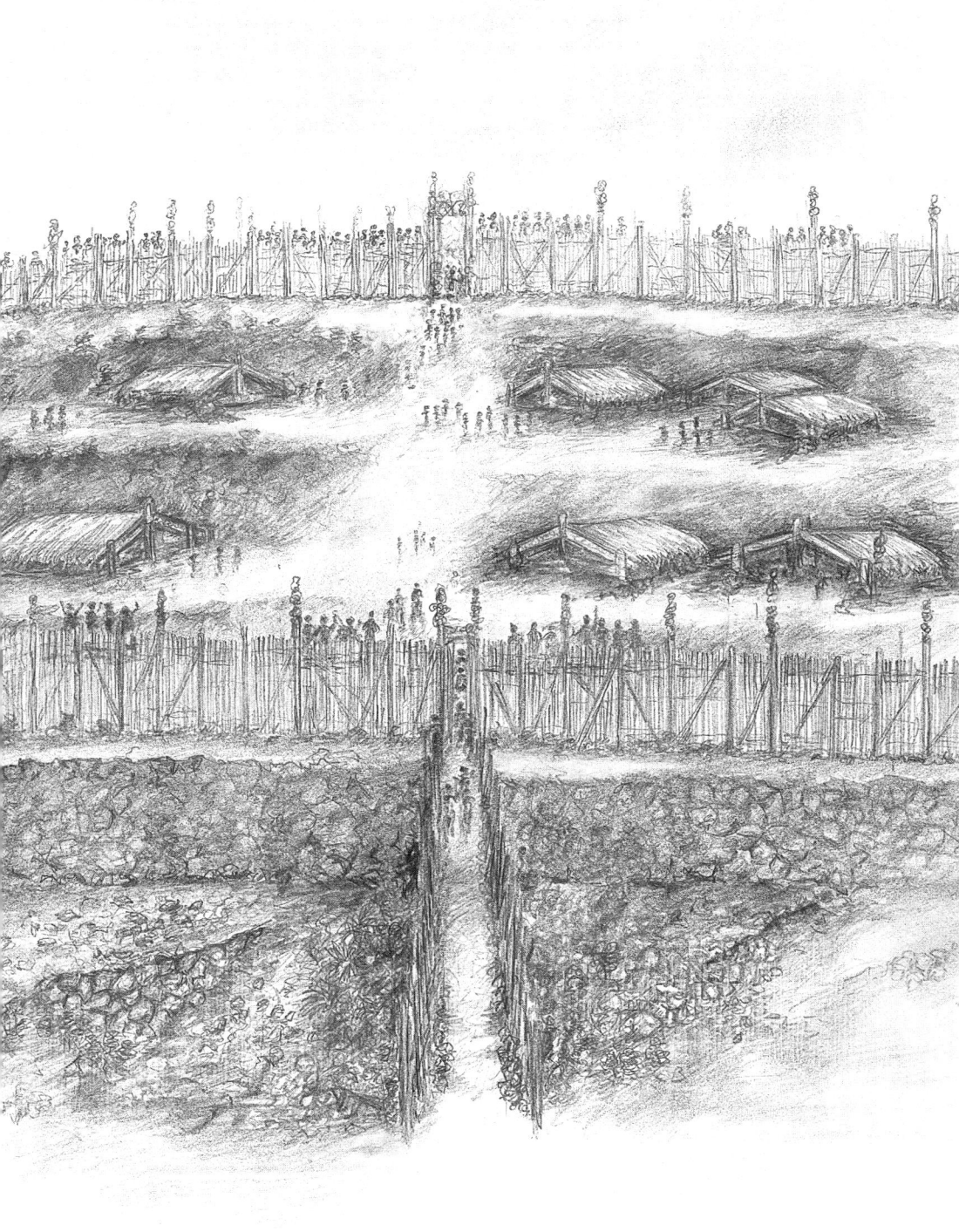

long spears (huata) which could be poked through the gaps in the palisades to reach those on the platforms.

About two-thirds of the way up the mountain was a wide terrace where huts were built, partly sunk into the ground. The people didn't have to worry about draining these pits because the scoria had plenty of holes in it, which allowed the water to seep away. These very low buildings, with the bank behind them, were well protected from the wind and quite cosy.

At the top of the mountain more huts were built in the craters. Some caverns were dug back into the hill to store water and food. The water had to be carried in gourds, and it then might have been poured into an old canoe for storage. The tribe only needed water for drinking as the hangi steamed the food and they washed in the sea.

Maungarei was very well defended, and the pa was alert at all times. This did not stop war parties attacking, however, and over and over again the warriors at the pa had to defend it. They were alert to Kawharu's taua when they came to attack. This warrior was fearless.

See also the story 'Raids, and More Raids', page 99.

Kawharu was a mythical giant chief of Ngati Whatua, reported to be seven metres tall. His taua used him as a human ladder.

At Pakuranga

Not far away, long before Kawharu came to Tamaki, there was a patupaiarehe war at Pakuranga. These fairies were from the Nukumaitore tribe. Putere was their leader and they fought the Koiwi. The fighting was going extremely badly for Putere and his taua, so to make the battle successful for them Putere chanted a special karakia. This made the sun (ra), which was beginning to set, stay motionless in the sky. Putere then instructed his taua to pluck the solid golden rays from the sun. Using these as spears they quickly overcame the Koiwi. After that day the hill was called Pakuranga-rahihi.

Maungawhau

The Giant Mataaho

When Mataaho, the giant god of the volcanoes, visited Aotearoa he felt the cold very badly as he was used to warmer countries. He called upon Mahuika, the fire goddess, to warm him. She responded by creating several volcanoes in the area, including Maungawhau. She also made the hot springs at Te Toangaroa, where Mataaho could soak until he was no longer cold.

Maungawhau has a large crater (called Te Ipu a Mataaho) which Mataaho used as his food bowl whenever he visited from the faraway countries. It was a very quiet, tapu place for him and many ceremonies were conducted there to make sure the volcano stayed asleep. Mataaho, being a giant, needed many slaves to prepare the food to fill this enormous bowl for him.

Some 19,000 years ago Maungawhau had erupted through three craters. Two of these filled up with the scoria fountaining from the third and deepest one, which exploded a bit later. About the time of Mataaho the patupaiarehe folk made a home on the mountain, but they did not return the day they failed to complete the bridge they were building at Meola (see 'The Patupaiarehe Bridge', page 73).

Despite it being tapu, the Maori people built a large pa on Maungawhau. The chief Titahi helped design the elaborate layout of the terraces and the extensive earthworks needed for these and the living areas. It was here that Kiwi Tamaki was born.

Near the mountain grew a sacred cabbage tree called Te Ti Tuhahi. This was a wahi tapu place where the umbilical cords of the children of the chieftains of the Waiohua tribe were buried. Tapu ceremonies were performed here each time a new child was born. At Te Ti Tuhahi a lovely waterfall fell away into a gully and flowed into the swampy countryside. On the mountainside itself there was and still is a large volcanic cavern.

Once, gardens circled the mountain. Each year a patch of lush bush was burned and a new garden planted. This way of gardening is called 'slash and burn'. Eventually the gardened area went right around the mountain. The areas that had been used for gardens previously, then left untouched for years, became desolate and stony, and only scrub and ferns grew there.

Near the mountain, at Te Ipu Pakore, the women went to collect fresh water in gourds. There was no spring or water on the mountain.

It was here at Te Ipu Pakore that the giant Kawharu, and his taua, killed some of these women. Nearby was Te Rereanga-ora-iti, where the survivors who had escaped from Kawharu leapt for their lives. Further away was a great swamp filled with cabbage trees. The water from this drained away into underground caverns, and it could be very dangerous for people travelling through this area. If they didn't fall into a bog they had to avoid the rocky outcrops that dotted the area, or they could become lost for days in the scrubby bushes.

There were two entrances to the Maungawhau pa. One was at Te Ngutu, the gate on the path to the spring, near which was Te Tuahu o Hua Kaiwaka shrine. Tapu ceremonies were frequently held here. On the other side of the mountain was the Arataki-haere path. This narrow track led from Maungawhau to Owhatihue where there was a small village. Here there was another tuahu place where tapu ceremonies were held.

At one time thousands of people lived on or near Maungawhau. They got their food from the sea and the large gardens. The men made their fishing floats from the cork-like bark of the whau tree. In time, however, the tribe joined the Waiohua for protection.

Te Ti Tuhahi was the Maori name for the area now known as Newmarket. In 1908 the sacred cabbage tree was chopped down by people from the school there. However, the stump of the tree was rescued and planted at Highwic, where some of its shoots have now grown into large trees.

Te Kawa-Iri-Rangi

The peace at Tamaki was often broken, and so it was that Te Kawa-Iri-Rangi, the eldest son of the great Maniopoto, married his cousin Hine-Kahukura as a way of strengthening the tribal links. This was in about 1625. Hine had four children, and then, sadly, she died. It often happened that people died young, as there were only tohunga to help with illnesses and other health problems.

In time Te Kawa heard that Hoki-Rau-Kawa had twin daughters who were very beautiful women. Hoki was an important Waiohua chief and a descendant of Hotoroa from the Tainui. Te Kawa went to Maungakiekie to visit Hoki, who agreed that he could marry the gorgeous twins. Having more than one wife was common if you were someone important.

Te Kawa's twin wives lived at Maungawhau, so he went to live with them there. He and his wives had two sons, then for some unknown reason Te Kawa's brother-in-law killed him. After this his two sons went to live with their father's tribe and became the leaders of the Maniopoto.

In the years that followed Te Kawa's murder there was just one attempt to seek utu, but it failed because the leader of the taua drowned in the Waikato River. Eventually, after several decades, Tutunui led a new Maniopoto taua on an expedition to seek utu. They travelled to Tamaki safely, and in the early morning mist they attacked at Maungakiekie.

Unfortunately Tutunui had a very loud voice, and the Waiohua heard him urging his men forward. Then, as the mist began to lift, they were able to see that Tutunui was actually quite a little man. They laughed at him and joked about his small size, which hurt his pride. This made him react rashly and he leapt forward ahead of his taua. The Waiohua quickly grabbed him and he was killed, then his body was hung in a karaka tree. His men promptly deserted and hurried home. So it was that Te Kawa's death was never properly avenged.

Ponga and Puhihuia

Ngati Kahukoka from Awhitu frequently waged war against the Waiohua. This was mostly because of disagreements over the shark-fishing grounds at Kauri Point. Then, when their old chief died, they decided to make peace, and in about 1650 a peace party of 30 men went to Maungawhau with their young chief Te Ponga. They took beautiful gifts of carved boxes, whalebone mere, woven mats, sharks' teeth and huia feathers.

The peace party was welcomed by the Waiohua, and the feasting, games, dances and haka went on for many days. During this time it was rumoured that Puhihuia, the granddaughter of Hotunui, was so impressed with Ponga's performance that she fell in love with him.

Puhihuia was the daughter of the chief Titahi of Maungawhau, and a hinepuhi — she had been chosen to marry someone very important. Because of this she and Ponga had to meet secretly, at night. One particular night, Ponga left the sleeping house, complaining that his slave was not near to bring him water. Puhihuia's mother was embarrassed when she heard their guest making such a fuss, and she sent Puhihuia to get water from the spring. Ponga was waiting for her in the darkness, and when they met they declared their love for each other. They decided to elope.

Ponga sent his slave ahead to the tauranga waka, to cut the ropes and lashings on the Waiohua canoes. Then Puhihuia hurriedly gathered up her slaves and possessions — cloaks, piupiu, her carved box of huia feathers, and her heru — and left with the 'peace party'. She dawdled a bit on the track, however, and had to hurry when her own people could be seen catching up.

Puhihuia's angry father desperately pursued the party through the valley below and down to the Manukau Harbour. But when Titahi's men quickly pushed out the canoes, they found that they fell to bits. Hurried repairs were made, and an urgently formed war party set out to get Puhihuia back. The fleeing couple were eventually caught at Whatipu. Here Puhihuia challenged the young wahine from her tribe to defeat her in hand-to-hand combat on the beach. As none of the six maidens she fought were able to beat her she won the right to leave with Ponga. Her father, Titahi, did not approve of this match to the young chief from out west, but he was unable to persuade her to return to her tribe. The peace agreement was over, however, and although both

Ponga and Puhihuia were descendants of Hotoroa from the *Tainui* canoe, the battles that followed were even more furious than before.

It did not help matters when a pet whale was encouraged to visit the Manukau. The people intended to give it as a gift to another tribe, but the Waiohua ambushed the whale and killed it, then they cooked and ate it. Eventually, however, peace was made and Ponga and Puhihuia lived happily together.

For many years the Waiohua tribe lived on at Maungawhau. Then, one day in about AD 1730, Rautao and his taua from Hauraki relentlessly attacked the pa and conquered the mountain. They did not stay there, however, and most of the Waiohua not killed in this fierce battle moved to Mangere to live. The pa soon became deserted as the few inhabitants who were left behind caught a dangerous illness and died.

See 'Kiwi and Rautao' (page 64) and 'Ureia the Taniwha' (page 16) for slightly different interpretations of these events.

Motuihe

Motu-a-Ihenga was named by Tuhoro, who was the son of Tamatekapua. Tuhoro named the island after his own son.

Rui Pungarehu

The patupaiarehe who used to live on Motuihe Island had been chased away and the chief Te-Ihu-Pare and his people had taken possession of the island. The ancient gardens on the island, which were called Muruiwi, were owned by Te-Ihu-Pare, and after his people had dug the soil he planted taro and hue. To guard the new plants as they grew he placed a carving of Ruru-tumaro (their owl guardian) in the garden.

One dark, foggy night, however, the patupaiarehe rowed their phantom canoes from Moehau and stole all of the newly ripe taro and hue. In fact it was not the crop itself that they stole, but the shape, or ahua. What they left appeared to be the real taro and hue, and the main core or matter, known as kaupapa, remained. But when the sun rose it heated up the plants, and as the day passed the whole crop shrivelled and dried up.

Te-Ihu-Pare knew it was the patupaiarehe who had done this terrible deed at his maara. He scolded Ruru-tumaro, who he had expected to take care of the crop. Ruru-tumaro sang in reply:

> The garden — the garden — shower it
> Shower it o'er with dust
> Shower it o'er with ashes
> Then will the food flourish
> And then all the fruits be saved
> Oh! Ooi Oh!

The next season a circle of ash fell around the garden, making an ambush the shape of a long jaw, or horseshoe, around it, but there was a gap where the patupaiarehe would be able to enter. When the new crop was ready another dark, foggy night fell over the island, and Ruru-tumaro called out:

> Oh the ambush trap — the long jaw
> Now shower it with the dust
> Now shower it with the ashes
> Now shower it o'er the gap of Ihupare
> Oh! Ooi — e!

Clouds of dust and ash fell all around, covering the gardens. Te-Ihu-Pare and his people fled, and it would be many days before they returned. The gardens on Motuihe were destroyed. This was the time when Rangitoto burst up from beneath the sea.

Hinerehia

Hinerehia was a patupaiarehe who lived on Motuihe. One day she was peacefully gathering rehia from the sea for food. When Karanga-roa, the Muruiwi chief, landed on the island he found her drying the seaweed in the sun at Ohinerehia. He was pleased to find such a fair maiden and captured her, then, not wasting any time, he married her. Soon he and Hinerehia had several fine sons and daughters.

Hinerehia was skilled in the arts and domestic duties of her patupaiarehe people. At night or on dreary foggy days she worked out of sight of the Muruiwi people. She would prepare, dye and weave flax into baskets and clothing and make other items to use or for decoration. Before the sun rose she would hide all her unfinished work. If she did not do this Tamatea-nui would undo all her work, and she would lose her ability to make such fine things if she disobeyed her people's customs. This is what she told the Muruiwi women, who were not happy that they were unable to learn these wonderful secret skills. Hinerehia called her ability 'ringa-matauranga'.

One day the Muruiwi women went to their tohunga to ask him to cast a spell on Hinerehia, to trick her into working in the daylight so that they would be able to watch and learn how she made everything. The tohunga worked his strong karakia and Hinerehia worked on into the day, not realising that the sun had risen, while the Muruiwi women hid where they could watch her.

As the day wore on Hinerehia became tired and the spell started to wear off. When she realised what had happened she was very upset, and she sang a mournful song of lament about having been deceived. As she sang a dense fog spread over Motuihe Island and concealed Hinerehia as she rose and travelled to Moehau. Her irirangi could be heard wailing to farewell her Muruiwi husband, Karanga-roa, and their children. They never saw her again, but in thick fogs or on dark nights when a death is near they sometimes hear her sad songs.

This was how the people of Motuihe learned the patupaiarehe weaving arts. To prevent the patupaiarehe stealing these skills back, all drying, dyeing and weaving must be done in the daylight and all work must be covered at night.

Ohinerangi

The Dwelling Place of Ohinerangi

At one time beautiful gardens surrounded Ohinerangi, but in time they were abandoned. Over the many years that followed, a rich forest of large trees grew there. Below the trees, lovely ferns sprouted and the birds came back to live. On the slopes, and beyond, karaka, puriri and pohutukawa grew, covering the area of Remuera and Orakei all the way to the Waitemata Harbour. The Maori people loved this area.

One day some Waiohua murdered and ate a young chieftainess from Hauraki. She was one of a party of visitors from Wharekawa. They cooked her, leaving her skirt on while she was in the oven, so that the hem of the skirt was scorched. Remu means the edge, and after this the area was named Remu-wera.

This murder had something to do with an earlier assassination of Kahurautao, his son Kiwi (this is not Kiwi Tamaki) and other Marutuahu chiefs. They had been in the Waikato area and were coming back by canoe. But after a visit to Maungawhau they were ambushed as they returned to their canoes at Tamaki. Because of this wicked deed the Mangawhau pa was besieged and conquered by Kahurautao's people.

The story of Ureia has a variation at what is now known as Remuera. This story tells us that the Waiohua were responsible for inviting Ureia to visit Haumia at Puponga Point, at the Manukau, and that it was they who killed and ate Ureia. They didn't use nets, and the taniwha came overland, not via Cape Reinga. It was because of this evil deed that Ngati Paoa from Hauraki set out to seek utu.

In fact Ngati Paoa used the death of Ureia as a reason to attack the Remu-wera pa. Following several marriages and skirmishes the Ngati Paoa had either lost or given away their very valuable greenstones. If a tribe gave away a greenstone it was usually a peace offering. Now Ngati Paoa decided they wanted their greenstone back, and the death of Ureia provided them with an opportunity — their taua would attack the Waiohua at Remu-wera.

Rautao was elected leader and he set off with his taua. Rautao had good reason to lead the attack because rebellious Waiohua had killed his father, Kahurautao, who had gone to get back his wife's greenstones. The Waiohua had also killed Rautao's brother, Kiwi, and hung the bodies in a puriri tree at Pututahi. Rautao now sought utu on behalf of these men.

See 'Wai-Puhi-Nui' and 'Kiwi and Rautao' in the Otahuhu section, pages 63 and 64, for variations on parts of this story.

Turanga and Pare-Huia — The Legend of Te Taurere

Near the west head of Tamaki was the fort of Taurere. Close to this a lush grove of karaka trees grew, and the people called this area Taurere.

Earlier, the Aotea canoe had reached Aotearoa, and the people of the canoe had visited Waitemata. They stayed at Taurere with the Ngati Titahi tribe who were living there, and were treated to feasting and dancing. Turi, a man from the Aotea canoe, had a son named Turanga-i-mua. Turanga was only a teenager but he fell in love with Pare-Huia, the beautiful young daughter of the chief Titahi. Tu gave her a present of karaka seeds, which came from Rangi-Tahua. At Turanga's request, Pare-Huia carefully planted the seeds near her home at Taurere.

Pare-Huia would one day be the wife of a chief, but this did not bother Turanga. When his people left to travel south he promised that he would return to marry Pare-Huia. He told her to look after the karaka trees, and that when they fruited he would return to Taurere.

Pare watered the seeds regularly and they began to grow. She was careful to take proper care of the little trees, and finally the spring season came when the trees, now fully grown, flowered and set berries. As the summer passed the berries ripened. Pare-Huia knew that soon Turanga-i-mua would come to get her.

Further south, at Patea, Turanga had grown into a fine warrior. He saw that the karaka nearby were fruiting, and he remembered his promise to Pare-Huia. He got together a group of friends so that he could travel safely to Tamaki. When he arrived at Taurere the tohunga welcomed him with the proper ceremonies, including the ceremony of tipi and atahu to be sure that the love of Tu and Pare would last. Now Tu and his party could enter the pa and be welcomed by Titahi with all the celebrations on the marae. Feasting, friendship and displays of skill in wielding the hoeroa were part of the merriment. Tu and his party showed how good they were at playing the games of niti and pere. Pare-Huia was charmed by Turanga as he was clearly the champion of the games.

After this the two lovers were seen together often, in and around the pa. Pare-Huia was more than happy to introduce Tu to all her friends and relatives, and she even took him to see the karaka trees with their first berries, now all very ripe.

Soon it was time for Turanga and his party to return home. Tu asked Titahi politely for Pare-Huia's hand in marriage. Unfortunately Titahi did not agree to this. Tu and his party left to visit relatives at the nearby One-pu-whakatakataka pa, where strong spells of atahu were chanted to make Pare flee her people to join Turanga. A very angry Titahi pursed her and ordered her to return home but Pare refused. A violent battle commenced, and before long the Ngati Titahi taua was defeated and Titahi himself lay dead.

Turanga and Pare, now his young wife, and their party quickly travelled south via the East Coast, then inland towards Taranaki. When they reached the Ruahine Range they had to fight an enemy taua and here Turanga was killed, despite having fought a successful battle. His party buried him nearby.

Near the battlefield Pare-Huia gave birth to their daughter, Ruahine. The survivors then travelled on to Patea. Old Turi mourned the loss of his son but welcomed his new daughter-in-law and his grandchild. Soon, however, Turi wandered off, broken-hearted from having lost his son. Some say he returned to Hawaiki.

Pare stayed there for many years but eventually she decided to return to her home at Taurere, leaving her daughter Ruahine with the Turanga people. Pare stayed on at Taurere for the rest of her life. When she died her body was placed, at her request, in a carved hakena and hung in the branches of one of her special karaka trees. She predicted that one day a pure white kotuku would appear at Waipuna. This would be a sign that her daughter was returning to Taurere.

Time passed, and one day a lovely kotuku was seen wading across the swamp that had formed from the freshwater spring which the Taurere people used. The tribe remembered Pare-Huia's ohaki and knew that Ruahine would soon return. They built an especially attractive house for her with newly woven mats.

Eventually the young chieftainess and her weary followers arrived. She was welcomed to the pa with all the traditional calling and powhiri, but first she visited her mother's remains, in the now sacred grove of karaka trees. When the grieving was complete Ruahine went into her new home and was warmly greeted by her mother's relatives. From here she chose her husband, and they and their children became the ancestors of many of the important chiefs of Tamaki. Near the ancient pa site the karaka trees still grow.

Otahuhu

Maramakikohura

Not long after the *Tainui* canoe arrived in Aotearoa the hapu set about exploring the Waitemata Harbour. The chief Hotoroa and all his wives except Maramakikohura, his beautiful second wife, were with those on the canoe when they arrived at Otahuhu. Before this Marama had asked to be put ashore at Wakatiwai, as she had decided she wanted somewhere comfortable to stay while the others explored. The long sea voyage on the canoe was enough for her.

A group of the tangata whenua at Wakatiwai took Marama to the Paretaiuru pa near the Hunua Range. Here, at the pa overlooking the Manukau, she was a celebrated guest. She conducted a sacred ceremony called uruuru whenua and claimed mana over the land.

Meanwhile those on the Tainui canoe rowed around Orere Point and through the Waiheke passage to Motukorea. They rested a while and then went on to Rangitoto. It was here that they met Tamatekapua on the Arawa. The Tainui rowed on to Te Kurae a Tura then, after exploring here, they travelled on to Te Haukapua. There was a dense fog here but the next day it cleared. Taiheku climbed Takarunga and from this high point he could see the Tamaki River and the Manukau Harbour.

The Tainui rowed on until they got as far as they could up the Tamaki estuary to Te Tauoma. They waited here for Marama to join them, but she and her companion Te Okaroa did not arrive at the arranged time. Taiheku, who had gone on ahead overland, had found a new stretch of water nearby and had seen the mullet jumping. He dipped his hands in the water and caught two of the fish easily.

The Tainui people laid down ponga log skids and tried to haul the large double-hulled canoe ashore. Powerful karakia were chanted by the tohunga, but the canoe stuck fast and would not move. This was Marama's fault. When she finally arrived Marama had to confess that she had committed adultery with Te Okaroa. After she had told them this Te Okaroa was violently killed, even though he was probably an important person in his tribe. The Tainui were then able to move the canoe straight away. They easily pushed the canoe across the narrow stretch of land (the portage), and from here the canoe glided gently into the Manukau Harbour. They set off once more to explore. Later the smaller hull of the Tainui was left at Motukorea.

Hotoroa's other wives, seeing Marama's sudden shame, took away all her fine clothes, leaving only the apron-like clothes worn by slaves and common people. Hotoroa forgave his favourite wife, but some time later when she gave birth to a child he was not sure the child was his, so Marama returned to Tamaki and settled on Puketutu Island. She called her son Motai.

Marama was later able to restore her mana. At Puketutu she founded the tribe called Nga Marama and several of these people became quite famous. The giant Kawharu was a descendant of Marama.

When Motai grew up he sought revenge from Hotoroa. His taua made a canoe at Rangiahua pa and set off after Hotoroa. The chief heard that they were coming and chanted spells that made the water rough on the bar at Aotea. A huge wave rolled over the canoe and all those on board perished.

The chief Hape was also on the *Tainui*, and he too returned to Tamaki. Although he had a club-foot he earned respect because he set up the skids at Maketu for the *Tainui* canoe. In time he went to live with Marama at Puketutu. When he died he was buried at Puketapapa. Many years later two ancient burial sites were excavated and it is almost certain that some of the old bones are Hape's. These were called Nga Tohu a *Tainui* (the sign of the Tainui).

Portages were where canoes had to be carried or hauled overland between two stretches of water. There was a portage at Papatoetoe that was two and a half kilometres long. The canoes had to be hauled uphill to a height of 20 metres above the sea. This allowed the tribes to put their canoes into the Waikato River, and the portage was also used by those travelling to Hauraki.

Two small islands at the Manukau end of the portage are called Te Tapotu O Tainui. Some say that when the skids of the Tainui were left here they formed these islands. Others claim that this was the last resting place of the skids.

Karanga-Hape means 'the calling of Hape'. Karangahape Road was part of a track that led all the way to Puponga. Karangahape was also the name for the area near Cornwallis. This name was given after Hape called out that Ureia, the taniwha, had been captured.

Canoe Highway

Right from the time of the first crossing by the Tainui canoe the portage at Otahuhu was a busy place. Thousands of canoes were dragged to and from both harbours. Having a portage at Otahuhu meant canoes did not need to be taken hundreds of kilometres around the top of New Zealand, in what was sometimes rough water, to get to this harbour. It also meant they did not have to cross the dangerous sandbar at the Manukau harbour's entrance to reach the plentiful fishing grounds. At Green Bay another portage was established and the canoes regularly went up and down the Whau creek, crossing from one harbour to the other.

Seabirds were easily caught at the Otahuhu portage. Because the time of the tides was different at each harbour the birds flew from one to the other between tides. Snares with nooses on tall poles were put up on the highest ridge at the portage. The birds were then frightened into these and caught as they crossed at the short cut. The tribes feasted on godwits, oystercatchers and other low-flying seabirds. Often the godwits were so fat and plentiful that they could be knocked to the ground using long forked sticks as they flew low over the portage.

The seabirds had a very strong fishy taste and many of them were quite small, but when there were several thousand people to feed, even a little meal was good. The tribes believed that if shags flew ahead of the incoming canoes it showed that others were approaching. They were then wary, as the visitors could be their enemies.

Most of the canoes that crossed the portages were light fishing vessels. A big waka was too heavy to shift this way, and it was not worth the effort to take it apart where it was lashed together for such a short journey. In the summertime hauling a canoe caused some problems as it was hard to get the canoe to slide along the worn dry track and the skids. In winter the canoes slid more easily over the soft ground, but the helpers often got cold and muddy. Getting around the isthmus by canoe was well worth the effort, however, as it was much faster than walking and there were no forests or swamps in the way.

Otahuhu was called 'the ridge-pole' because, like the ridge-pole in a house, it divides. Otahuhu divided the Waitemata Harbour from the Manukau Harbour. The name Otahuhu had nothing to do with the huhu grub. Reipae of Ngati Paoa married the chief Tahuhunui, who was a Ngai Tahuhu. In time Tahuhunui found his way to this area and made a strong pa at Te pa o Tahuhu. The pa was heavily fortified as all the tribes travelling north and south passed this way. The Tahuhu people were related to the Waiohua, yet the portage for the canoes became known as Otahuhu.

On and around Te pa o Tahuhu there were huge gardens. The tribe found large green sphinx moth caterpillars on the kumara leaves, and these were collected and eaten. The pa had some of the biggest kumara pits to be seen. The little extinct volcano nearby, at what we now call Sturges Park, also had extensive gardens around the crater, which was filled with swampy mud and plants. Many people worked in these gardens and their skeletons have been found nearby.

The Ngai Tahuhu tribe often lived at other places. After the gardens were planted they went away to catch fish and eels and to gather shellfish. They would also be busy building new terraces on the mountain at Te pa o Tahuhu for new whare and storehouses. One day they were visited by their enemies, the Tauoma. These people practised witchcraft, and it was the spells they chanted that killed the chief Tahuhu. After the tangi and burial, some of Tahuhu's people went to live up north. Some mixed with the other tribes in the area, and the pa was abandoned. The Te Toko Tu Whenua or Rongo stone that was in the garden was taken to Te Tatua a Riukiuta. Otahuhu became a tapu area.

In time Ngati Paoa of Hauraki came to settle here, and the Ngai Tahuhu people gave a chief's daughter and a greenstone mere to the Hauraki tribe to gain protection for the tribe. But over time the local tribes mounted many war expeditions against the Ngati Paoa, and many of them were killed in battle. The Ngati Paoa moved away from Otahuhu, although they still owned the area. About the same time as this, Ngati Whatua and Te Atita murdered the Nga Puhi chief Koperu in this neighbourhood.

The land crossing at Otahuhu was only about 700 metres long. The portage at Green Bay, which was not much longer, was to be made into a proper canal but this never happened. It would have gone along Canal Road in Avondale and up Portage Road. When the Maori people used the portage the Whau creek went a lot further towards Green Bay. This has now been piped and filled in, which is a pity — think of the practical use and fun this would have been, even if a toll had been charged to take your boat through the canal. Even today the birds cross the portages at the change of tides, although there are not as many birds as there used to be.

No one is really sure where the stone at Te pa o Tahuhu went. It also was a Rongo stone. It is possible that Te Tatua a Riukiuta was part of the Three Kings, possibly the garden there. Tatua is part of the name of one of that group of mountains. The gardens at Three Kings had individual names.

Puketutu

This island was first called Motu-o-Hiaroa. Many people lived here, gardening and fishing, and they divided the lovely island up between each hapu. Because it was partly isolated from the surrounding areas the island was easily fortified with rock walls and terraces. In time, however, there were too many people living on the island so they moved to the mainland. Puketutu became a sacred place and the tohunga made it their home. No one dared to disobey them.

For as long as anyone can remember, Patara te Tuhi was the tuahu on Puketutu. As a sacred place it had great mana. There was a raised flat area at the top of the highest point on Puketutu, and this place was called Taumata-o-Rakataura. Rakataura was a powerful tohunga who came from the Tainui canoe. He was the brother of Hiaroa, and he settled at Puketutu with the Nga Oho people.

Rakataura was courting Kahurere, Hoturoa's lovely daughter. Hoturoa was far from pleased about this and he did his best to stop the two marrying, but Rakataura would not be discouraged.

In another version of why the *Tainui* got stuck on its skids, Rakataura became annoyed with some of the rowers on the *Tainui* canoe, so at the tuahu he chanted a karakia that stopped the *Tainui* from sliding on its skids from Otahuhu into the Manukau. When Hiaroa, his brother, complained bitterly, Rakataura crossed over to the Otahuhu side and used other karakia to allow the canoe to move.

Puketapapa Pa

The Puketapapa pa on Puketutu was special because its strong double palisades were tied together underground to heavy stringers. The Nga Oho descendants of Ohomairangi, from the *Arawa* canoe, lived here. As the centuries passed many a bloody battle took place to try to gain possession of Puketutu Island.

Around 1750 Ngati Whatua led by Te Waha-akiaki attacked at Te One-rangaa but were forced back. They then decided to camp on the opposite shore at Te Aratahuna to stop anyone escaping across the sandspit. It wasn't long before the people at Puketapapa pa were out of water and thirsty.

One night the chiefs decided the tribe would creep away and off the island to seek the safety of the Mangere pa. The Ngati Whatua found out and attacked them, and after much loss of life on both sides the people of Puketapapa drove their enemies away. The survivors of the battle made it to the safety of the Mangere pa, and not long after this the island became deserted.

Puketapapa was also the name for Mt Roskill.

Wai-Puhi-Nui

Wars were raging between the Waiohua and the Hauraki tribes. As both adversaries were rather tired of fighting they decided to make peace, and a party of Hauraki chiefs were invited to visit the Tamaki people. While the chiefs were visiting, their crews hauled their canoes across the portage.

As the chiefs were returning to their canoes they were ambushed by the Maungawhau people they had just been visiting, and most of them were cruelly murdered. Among the survivors was Rautao, who was able to gather his remaining people together and escape on a large canoe that was still on the other side of the portage. The name of this canoe was Puhinui.

Rautao's brother Kiwi had married a Waikato chieftainess, and it was her people who had given the Puhinui to the Hauraki tribe as a wedding present. Because Rautao had only a few men to help, moving the big canoe was very difficult, so he decided to hide it in the creek (now named Puhinui Creek) until it was safe to leave. Later the party returned to Hauraki, where Rautao told his people of the disaster. A war party was organised to seek utu for the murders. The women packed good supplies of food for the warriors, who travelled by land and sea to reach Otahuhu.

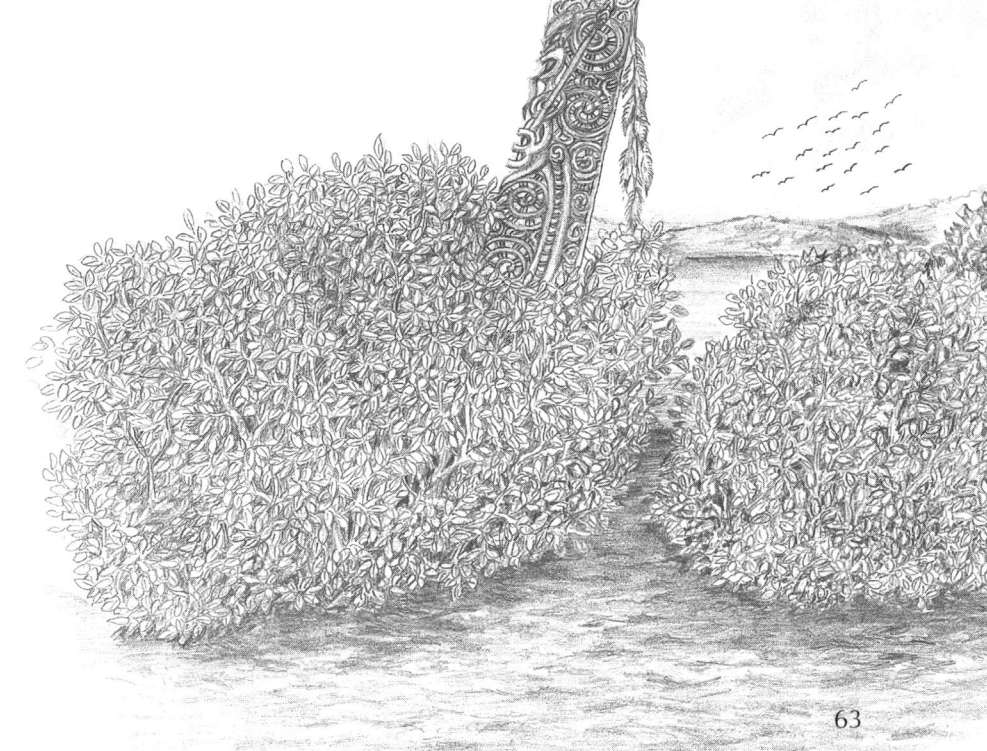

The first task was to hide the Puhinui in the creek again. Later Rautao sent out his spies, who came back to report that the Waiohua had found the canoe and were dragging it into the deeper water. They were singing an insulting canoe-hauling song which told Rautao's spies that they had found the canoe because the feather plumes were visible above the mangroves. Rautao had forgotten to take these off. But the Waiohua were so busy capturing the Puhinui as their prize that they did not notice the Hauraki taua approaching. They were surprised by the sudden attack and defeated, and so Rautao got the precious canoe back.

Kiwi and Rautao

Kahurautao, a Hauraki chief, had two sons, Rautao and Kiwi. Not long after the killing of Ureia, Kahurautao travelled to the Waikato with his son Kiwi to receive a wedding gift, a pataka, from Kiwi's wife's people. It was a carved storehouse that had to be taken apart so that it would fit into the canoe. Kahurautao and his paddlers then returned to Tamaki by crossing at the Awaroa portage, which linked the Waikato River to Waiuku, then crossing from the Manukau to the Tamaki River at the Karetu portage. Although this was a more difficult route than the Otahuhu portage it was chosen because Kahu and Kiwi planned to visit the Waiohua on the way home.

At Pukaki in Mangere the Waiohua promised to give them a greenstone mere and a heitiki to make amends for killing the Hauraki people's beloved taniwha Ureia. The guests were warmly welcomed and a feast prepared in their honour. The gifts were then presented and everyone retired for the night, as the Hauraki were leaving early the next morning.

The Waiohua, however, already regretted their generosity, and had planned beforehand to murder their guests. But they did not want to be blamed for such a crime, and they did not want the Hauraki tribe to seek utu. So the crafty Waiohua told Kahurautao and Kiwi to travel with their party to Maungawhau, where they would receive more gifts. Unsuspecting, Kahu's group set off. Once again they were greeted by 'friendly' hosts, and they thanked the Waiohua for the wonderful presents. They then said their good-byes and set off, unaware that a taua would be waiting for them on the track they had to use when they returned to their canoe at Tamaki.

The evil ambush was at Te Kopuke. The Waiohua murderers rushed from their hiding place beside the track and killed both Kahurautao and Kiwi. The bodies were hung in a puriri tree at Orere. The place where the murders took place was from then on known as Patutahi.

It took some time before news of this wicked event reached Kahurautao's other two sons. Rautao, the eldest son, then married Kiwi's wife, as was the custom. It was a long time before Rautao retaliated and utu for the double murder was settled.

Much later Rautao raised a taua and set off after the Waiohua. The first group he attacked was a subtribe of the Waiohua at Wairoa. None of these people had anything to do with the crime but Maori utu blames anyone related to the murderer. Rautao's taua killed many and the others fled in all directions. Rautao didn't waste any time, crossing quickly to Waiheke where he conquered the Ngati Huarere, who were also a subtribe of the Waiohua. The taua then headed up the Tamaki River and conquered the Taurere and Mokoia pa.

At Maungarei Rautao sent his scouts out around the base of the mountain. They discovered that the pa was watchful and had a full-strength group of warriors guarding it, so he decided not to attack. A little way to the southeast of the pa Rautao found an unsuspecting group of people sunbathing. His taua pounced on these people and killed them all. Feeling very powerful, Rautao then led his taua back to attack Maungarei. So fierce were they that they soon conquered the pa. Rautao really blamed the Maungawhau tribes for the murder of his father and brother, and so relentless was the attack there that the inhabitants who survived left and never returned. Some went to live at Maungakiekie. Eventually the Waiohua made peace with Rautao, and to seal the bargain they gave him an attractive wife from the Wairoa subtribe.

Owairaka

Wairaka

In the days before the coming of the Matatua canoe, there lived a remarkable woman called Wairaka. She was the beautiful, rebellious daughter of the Ngati Awa chief Toroa.

Wairaka lived on the wonderful sun-drenched, palm-fringed island of Tahiti. Most days a fair-sized surf rolled in on the main beach. Wairaka was a very good swimmer, and she developed a craze for surfboard riding. She became very skilled at this sport and often rode the huge waves to satisfy her adventurous spirit.

In time Wairaka married. Her new husband decided that her love of surfing was not suitable for a married woman, and to discourage her he moved her to an inland village. But Wairaka did not wish to give up her sport, and she often made the long journey to the sea. Her husband became so annoyed that he beat her cruelly.

This was not an acceptable punishment for the daughter of a chief. After all, she had not done anything really wrong. Toroa, Wairaka's father, became angry and argued with her husband's family. A bitter feud developed. Life became uncomfortable for all, whereupon Toroa, Wairaka and his people left Tahiti for good, bound for the legendary Aotearoa.

After many months, guided only by the stars, and running short of food and water, this group of weary travellers finally made landfall at Whakatane. Shortly afterwards the men went ashore to check the area and seek food and fresh water. While they were away the canoe with the women on board began to drift out to sea. Although it is traditional for the men only to paddle the large war canoes, Wairaka, seeing the peril they were in, and ignoring her position as a chief's daughter, called, 'Ka Whakatane aki au i ahau' — 'I will make myself act like a man.'

The clumsy paddles were seized, and with the help of the other women Wairaka brought the heavy canoe safely to shore.

The tribe settled in the Bay of Plenty, establishing villages and large, productive gardens. Toroa then decided it was time his daughter selected a new husband — her strong nature meant that she might not agree with any choice her father made.

Against her father's wishes Wairaka had decided that Toko, a handsome warrior, was the man she wished to marry.

So that her choice would have to be accepted, one moonless night she crept into the whare where Toko slept. She lay beside him then, needing to produce evidence of this, she scratched his face. In the early dawn Wairaka emerged to announce her chosen husband. Alas, it was not Toko's face that was scratched but that of Mai-ure-nui, a much older man whose face was scarred and ugly. Mai-ure-nui had seen the secret glances Wairaka bestowed upon Toko, and had changed sleeping places the night before. Wairaka's father insisted that the marriage ceremony should take place, even though Wairaka wailed with dismay. There is an old saying that says, 'It was by darkness Wairaka was misled.'

Being a strong-minded woman, Wairaka would not accept her fate. Within days she had quietly organised a travelling party. They left in the dead of night and travelled swiftly northward. After many weeks they came to a hill which they named Te Puke o Wairaka. Wairaka lit a huge fire on the mountaintop to let everyone know that she had chosen this place to be her home. Here the people formed a new community. Wairaka made a new beginning and found a new husband who treated her well, and with whom she lived happily.

Ruarangi

Many years ago the place we now know as Mt Albert was the site of a strongly fortified pa. The mountain was called Te Puke o Ruarangi, meaning the hill of Ruarangi, before it became known as Te Puke o Wairaka. Ruarangi, who was rather fat, was the chief of the tribe. Many long and bitter battles had been won at this pa.

Beneath the pa, on the southern side, was the opening to a large volcanic cavern formed in the days when Ruaumoko (the god of earthquakes) visited the region and called on Mahuika (the fire goddess) to warm him. So successful was the volcanic activity that a mountain heaved from the earth, gushing fire and lava. Within this a gigantic gas pocket, now called Ruarangi's Cave, formed. Large enough to shelter 700 people in its first cavern, it sank darkly under the mountain. The people believed this underground passage of black rock, and even blacker sticky wet soil, stretched all the way to Western Springs.

One unfortunate day, after many weeks of being fiercely besieged by a war party from Thames, Ruarangi's people were cut off from the water and freedom. The battle raged on endlessly and defeat was near for those in the hill pa. While the tribal warriors held off their attackers on the battlements Ruarangi called a hasty meeting of his people. An escape route was planned.

While the war party was kept busy on the north side of the pa, the last remnants of the tribe began a desperate scramble over rocky outcrops and around scrubby mountain bushes to the cave. Once they were safely inside, the flax torches that were stored there for emergencies were quickly lit to illuminate the eternal darkness. So began the desperate journey to freedom.

Stepping from rock to rock, the tribe made their way some distance inside the cave, until they came to a place where the sides closed in, leaving only a narrow opening. Carefully all but one managed to squeeze through and escape to safety. Left behind was Ruarangi himself, defeated by his immense size. No matter how he tried he could not pass, and to this day the cave is known as Te-Ara-Tomo-o-Ruarangi (the cave path of Ruarangi).

The Patupaiarehe Bridge

High on the misty tops of the forest-clad hills in several parts of the North Island lived the patupaiarehe, or fairy people. They were fair of skin and hair, dressed in filmy white clothes, with not a tattoo on their delicate faces. Most were small in size and not likely to be seen by passing humans, for they possessed supernatural powers and were able to become invisible. They only ventured out at night or on dull, cloudy days, so they became known as 'the children of the mist'.

Many patupaiarehe were feared, for it was said that they lured men and women to destruction with the ghostly music they played on their flutes. Strange uncanny sounds from the bush were feared as the work of these fairy people. Often the patupaiarehe came down from the hills in the dim, misty weather to fish for eels and the little fish called upokororo.

One such group from Hunua were not unlike the sea-fairies, with whom they shared a fear of sunlight. This group of patupaiarehe had travelled northward searching for new fishing grounds. They had passed through Papakura and crossed the narrow strip of land dividing the Waitemata and Manukau harbours, but when they arrived at the upper reaches of the Waitemata their path was blocked by its waters. Fortunately there was an extremely low tide so, undeterred, the patupaiarehe set to work in the darkness, furiously building a stone causeway across the harbour.

Normally the patupaiarehe can successfully complete their tasks in one night, but unfortunately the causeway proved to be a challenge beyond their ability. The new day dawned long before the task was done, so the work was left unfinished. The patupaiarehe fled and never returned. To this day, the patupaiarehe 'bridge' can be traced at low tide from Te Tatua a Riukiuta, where the lava flowed out into the Waitemata Harbour at Meola Reef.

It is now believed that the reef was actually formed from a lava flow from the Three Kings volcano some 20,000 years ago. Today known as The Black Reef, earlier names were Te Tokaroa (the long reef) and Te Ara Whakapekapeka a Ruarangi (the perplexing pathway of Ruarangi). You can see this reef clearly from the top of Mt Albert when the tide is out. It stretches nearly two-thirds of the way across the Waitemata Harbour towards Birkenhead.

The names for Three Kings were Koheraunui (The Big King), Te Tatua a Mataaho (Centre King) and Taurangi (South King).

Rangitoto

Rangitoto, which is also said to be named after Rangi and Papa, is a 'shield mountain', with its high buttress at the top and ragged, rocky valleys. These valleys are dangerous to anyone who strays from the tracks. The lava that flowed from below formed three caverns. No water stays on the surface of this island, but it sinks deep underground into a huge rocky subterranean reservoir. Here the pure fresh water is permanently trapped.

Rangitoto is the only volcano in the area that was born from beneath the sea. Geologically it is a very young volcano, and the last one to blow. It remained a jagged, rocky and soil-less mountain beneath its scanty covering of scrub. The slow process of weathering from the rains and the wind will take many thousands of years.

For many years after the emergence of Rangitoto nothing grew there. Then, one spring, Karoro, a black-backed gull, asked the mountain if it could rest there. Soon many gulls began resting there — the akiakei, the tara, and the migratory birds that passed on their flights north and south.

One day Riroriro visited and brought a few seeds. Soon other birds brought seeds. As there was no soil, the seeds sprouted in the few crevices where plants could start growing. Over the years more plants grew in the leaf litter under the little trees. A piwakawaka flew over from the mainland and found a few insects among the stubby bushes. Soon other fantails came to chirp and flit about with all the other birds.

Today everyone can see Rangitoto from all over Auckland. Ruaumoko called it Rangitoto Tu-Mata-Uenga — the last born of the volcanoes. The low bush is now becoming lush and dense, and other birds now live happily in the larger trees. Our country's rare prehistoric living fossil, the fork fern, Psilotum nudum, and the delicate translucent kidney fern, can be found there among the common plants we see elsewhere in New Zealand.

At one time Peretu, the chief of the Rahopara pa, owned Rangitoto. He had a rahui kaka (a parrot reserve) there. The volcano was also a wonderful lookout for the tribe.

The Turehu Myth

Every once in a while the Turehu tohunga would meet on a hill named Te Ahuahu. This place was just northwest of Tahoro Bay on the west coast. It was here that they practised their wananga and acted out the sacred rituals. Traditional Maori lore was discussed, and they gave demonstrations of their spiritual powers to show each other what they could do. Sometimes their power went much too far and a large part of the landscape changed its shape quite dramatically. They would say this was an accident.

One particular day, a tohunga called Takamiro took off his maro (girdle or apron) with a flourish and tossed it high into the air. The wind carried it south and it landed at Whatipu. Here it turned into the rock now known as Marotiri.

Tiriwa, the Turehu chieftain, did not like to be outdone. To demonstrate that his supernatural powers were superior, he decided to shift Rangitoto. The mountain was spoiling the view for those who were at Te Ahuahu that day — they couldn't see the coast from there, or the Manukau Heads.

Tiriwa strode over to the volcano and chanted karakia to lighten its immense weight. He was then able to lift the mountain onto his shoulders and carry it away. With his huge strides he carried the mountain east over the Waitakeres to the Waitemata Harbour. Then he began to carry the volcano out to sea. The water was very cold and Tiriwa gasped as it rose up his thighs. This caused him to drop Rangitoto in the place where it is found today, in the sea at the entrance to the Waitemata.

Matakamokamo and Matakerepo

One sultry morning some 600 years ago a rosy dawn broke over the Tamaki isthmus. Volcanic eruptions thousands of years earlier had buried most of the lush kauri forest, but patches still grew around the countryside. On that day no birdsong was heard in the forest, but no one noticed the silence across the land.

Matakerepo, the wife of the chief Matakamokamo, had been working on a new cloak for her husband for many months, and today she would finish it. Some say that these two and their children were from a family of giants who were the children of the fire gods. Their hair was long and tangled, and they had enormous bulging eyes that gleamed with the colours of the paua shells.

While the rest of the tribe at Te Rua Maunga busied themselves with their daily chores and the women set about preparing food for the hangi, Matakerepo got on with her work. She was too occupied to take any notice of the menfolk pushing out their canoes to go fishing at the nearby fishing ground. Much of the food they ate came from the prolific fishing spot they rowed to. Here the nets were set and the bone-hooked fishing lines were tossed overboard.

As the day passed Matakerepo worked diligently. She wove and knotted, and added some kiwi feathers to make the cloak warm. It was late afternoon when she realised that she would not finish her work that day. Then Matakamokamo decided he did not like his new cloak, and argued loudly with his wife. Slowly the light faded and darkness settled over the land. No birds were chirping in the forest. Matakerepo had not noticed the lack of birdsong, nor had she noticed that their fire had gone out. When she realised this she was so annoyed she cursed Mahuika, the goddess of fire, for letting this happen. Matakamokamo cursed too because he was cold.

Mahuika heard them and rose grumpily. How dare they call for the assistance of such a powerful goddess. Instead of coming to their aid Mahuika asked for help from Mataaho to send a volcanic eruption to punish the quarrelling couple.

Suddenly the birds set up a wild, fearful squawking and frantically flew away to the inland forest. The ground trembled violently and a gigantic hole appeared at Te Rua Maunga as Mataaho sucked the ground away.

Water filled the hole and Lake Pupuke was born. Out at sea Rangitoto pushed up into the harbour.

Matakamokamo and Matakerepo were so afraid that they fled with their slave Takiata to Rangitoto. They were in such a hurry that they left their twin children behind at Waiwharariki, and Takiata was ordered to rescue them. She was told to keep looking downwards so she would not anger Mataaho. Unfortunately she forgot her instructions, and both she and the twins, Hinerei and Matamiha, were turned to stone at the southern end of Waiwharariki.

Matakamokamo and Matakerepo then returned to the mainland, but they too were turned to stone by Mataaho. This set off more volcanic eruptions, which exploded at Te Kopua o Matakerepo and at Te Kopua o Matakamokamo. The three peaks on Rangitoto represent these two and their slave. When the mist forms over Rangitoto people say that Matakamokamo and Matakerepo are weeping for their children and their lost home.

Lake Pupuke is an explosion volcano. This explains why it is deep and not very high.

Island of the Bloody Skies

In the middle of the Waitemata Harbour the sea boiled and fire heaved itself skywards. The sky itself turned blood-red. As Rangitoto emerged dramatically hot and fiery from the seabed, massive shockwaves rocked the area. The men of the tribe rushed desperately to rescue their canoes and other items that were being dashed on the shore. They now knew why the birds had been silent.

The eruption quietened but the mountain still glowed red on the horizon. It took many weeks for it to cool to a stark, dark-brown island. In the time that Rangitoto glowed in the dark it was watched over by Marama (the moon) but was hidden from the view of those who lived in the ancient pa at Orakei.

Tamatekapua, the captain of the Arawa canoe, and others in the Great Fleet were guided by the light and smoke from the volcano when bringing the canoes to Aotearoa. It was here that the Tainui and the Arawa met. Tamatekapua made improper advances to Whakaotirangi, who was Hoturoa's first wife, and this started a fierce battle at Oruawharu (Islington Bay). Tamatekapua was badly wounded and retreated to Rangitoto, where he cut his feet on the sharp scoria. He bled so much from his cuts and wounds that the rocks were stained red. To this day you can find the red rocks on the island. The scoria is still very sharp. Be warned: do not wander barefoot on Rangitoto or your blood too will stain the rocks.

The name Te Rangi-i-totonga-a-Tamatekapua means 'the days of bleeding of Tamatekapua'.

Manawatere

Manawatere came from Hawaiki in a magical way. Without a canoe he surfed over the waves and landed at Maraetai. From here he travelled to the Orawaho passageway, between Rangitoto and Motutapu islands, but he did not know the right karakia to quieten the lizard guardians Moko-nui-o-Kahu and Moko-nui-o-Hei. When he tried to swim through the narrow passage the lizards caused the sea to be so rough that he drowned. The moral here is that even if you are a very good swimmer local knowledge is very important.

Motutapu

It was either Hoturoa or Taiheku from the *Tainui* canoe who named this island Te Motutapu a Tinirau. Earlier people had settled in the bays and the dense forests of Tane. The birds were plentiful and fish teemed in the sea around the island.

Fortunately no people were on the island on the fateful day when Rangitoto rose from the sea right next to Motutapu. They had gone to the mainland in search of food. Motutapu was covered in fiery grit which burnt the forests and the villages to the ground. No gardens remained. When the people returned Motutapu was a very different island. It looked like a moonscape. Although the early Maori settlement disappeared, beneath the grit and ash can be found the footprints of these people and the bones of rare or extinct birds. These include the moa, the crow and the eagle.

Most of the people who had lived on Motutapu moved to various places on the Tamaki isthmus to begin new gardens and make new pa sites on the extinct volcanoes. In later years they returned to collect stone from Motutapu to make their adzes. In time Ngati Huarere settled on Motutapu and nearby Motuihe.

Te Haukupua and Rahopara

In the Beginning

Kui grew up on Te Ika a Maui, and his people, Ngati Kui, lived there for many years.

One day new people, the Tutumaio, came from far away and landed on Te Ika roa a Maui. As soon as they realised that others lived here they started fighting them. Using their cunning, they defeated the Ngati Kui, and soon they ruled the land. The Ngati Kui who died went down under the earth to live, and the Tutumaio married those who were still alive. For many years they ruled the land.

Much later a party of Turehu arrived from a faraway land. War broke out between the Tutumaio and the Turehu as soon as they landed. The Turehu used their weapons and they too were cunning, and so they won the war with the Tutumaio. They married the surviving men and women of the Tutumaio, who became Turehu. Soon the Tutumaio were said to be extinct, and the Turehu ruled the land.

For many years the Turehu lived in Te Ika a Maui, then once again a party came from far away. These people were descendants of Maui and they were looking for the fish of their ancestor. These people were Maori, and they wished to settle on Te Ika a Maui.

When the Maori found the Turehu here they began a war using their weapons. They were even more cunning than the Turehu and they won the battle. Again, they married the survivors, and the land was ruled by the Maori. After they had borne many children there were thousands of Maori people. Now, 46 generations later, Te Ika a Maui belongs to the descendants of this tribe.

The people of Ngati Kui, the Tutumaio and the Turehu are no more. Tutumaio, however, sometimes appears as a ghost in people's eyes, but if they try too hard to see him he disappears. The Turehu became like the patupaiarehe, and like these fairy folk, their spirit and voices can be heard on misty days deep in the forest. But the Turehu angered the god Io, and because of this they disappeared and only monsters (tapua) were left. This was the curse of Io. Then the tapua lit cooking fires and cooked their mother. They ate the fat and flesh of their mother. This poisoned them, so they too all disappeared.

Te Haukupua

At the time of the Great Fleet the *Tainui* canoe explored much of the coastline of Aotearoa. Not knowing where they were going, they had to be fairly careful. In time they visited Te Haukapua. Some time after this they rowed around to the sandspit which became known as Rangi o Taiheku after their canoe got stuck here. Now, it's not a good idea to get a large waka stuck anywhere. It takes a lot of hard work and many men to move a waterlogged canoe back into the water. Taiheku swam ashore, probably trying to get help, but hardly anyone lived in the area.

People settled at Maungauika and built a great pa on the hilltop. This pa stood guard over anyone entering the Waitemata Harbour. It was a very valuable fortress to the people of Uika. Later, Ngati Paoa from Hauraki got control of all the islands and came up the Awanui o Perehu to attack the Kawerau.

Rahopara

About 100,000 years ago Lake Pupuke erupted and the lava from the volcano flowed through a lush kauri forest. The lava cooled around the trees, and they slowly burned away from within. This left the imprints of these huge trees in the reef at Takapuna Beach.

Nearby was a pleasant grassy headland studded with trees. This was the site of Rahopara pa. At first many people lived at the pa, and the tribe depended on its natural defences. There were steep cliffs on the beach side and a huge natural ditch that protected it from enemy tribes approaching overland. This ditch was steep, and it was 12 metres wide and 12 metres deep. The tribe only needed a few simple terraces along the ditch. In prehistoric times there was a river here.

Not far from the pa, near Maungauika, was the cave called Te Ana o Kahumauroa. When Ngati Paoa attacked the Takapuna pa Nga Puhi captured their canoe, Kahumauroa, and hid it in this cave. High up on the bank the chief Taramokomoko defended the last attack on the pa, which was led by his brother-in-law, the chief Kapetawa. This raid was successful, and after this battle the pa became a deserted ruin.

See also the Waiheke stories, such as 'Kapetawa', for more on this area.

The Kawerau

Maki of Ngati Awa

From Taranaki came Maki. He had an influence on many places on the Tamaki isthmus and was responsible for the forming of the Kawerau tribe.

Rarotonga

Often a chief would ask for help from another tribe. One time when the chief Hauparoa was being threatened by Ngati Whatua he asked Maki to help. Maki agreed but was in no hurry to arrive at the meeting place. He took his time, and when he reached Manurewa, as the tribe there did not object, he decided to stay a few days to rest.

While Maki was staying there the chief Taihua, from the Takapuna pa, came to Manurewa and claimed that Maki was a relative of his. Before Taihua met Maki he left a bowl hidden in the scrub nearby. During the night some warriors from Rarotonga killed Taihua's son and placed the boy's heart in the bowl. When Taihua later sent his slave to bring the bowl back to him he found his son's heart.

He then did a very strange thing. He took the heart out and tied it on a string, and threw it at the sleeping Maki. Maki, who was still tired from the previous night's socialising, awoke and grabbed at it but Taihua quickly pulled it back. He threw it again, and again pulled it back. The next time he threw it Maki was ready and caught the heart. Once Taihua saw that Maki had a firm hold on the heart he told him that it was his son's. Maki painted the bowl red and placed the heart in it. When this was done he wanted to know who had done this terrible deed, as Taihua's son was also a relative of his.

Maki and Taihua planned utu and gathered together their people. Then they disguised themselves and set off to Rarotonga, where they found the people working in their garden below their mountain pa. Maki's people took a ko each and started to help with planting the kumara. Then, at a pre-arranged signal, Maki's men threw off their cloaks, revealing their weapons, and killed all the Rarotonga people. The murder of Taihua's son was avenged. This battle has two names: Te Ipu Kura a Maki (the red bowl of Maki) and Te Waewae Kotuku (the heron's foot).

In another version of this story Maki and his supporters travelled to an area close to Manurewa. Here they settled for a while with the Waiohua chief Whauwhau and his whanau. Not long after Maki arrived there a distant relative of his, Taihua, who originally came from Taranaki, arrived from Takapuna. His son had just been murdered on the track leading south from Koheraunui to Rarotonga. Taihua had come to seek utu.

After a meeting with Whauwhau, Maki was asked to go to Waipuna to help cultivate the garden there. Maki agreed and told the men to sharpen their ko at both ends for the digging. He also instructed them to tie the footrests with slip-knots so that they could be quickly removed.

When everything was ready Whauwhau, Maki, Taihua and their war party travelled to the spring at Waipuna, on the western side of the Panmure Basin. Soon they were all busy digging, but it was not long before Maki and his followers started an argument. Shortly after that Whauwhau's followers decided it was time to eat. At this moment Maki shouted, 'Remove your footrests! Attack! Kill them!' Maki had decided that he wanted the land for himself.

Wielding the sharpened ends of their ko handles as spears, they soon killed all the Whauwhau. This incident was called Waewae-kotuku, because of the way the footrests were attached to the ko handles.

At Kauri Point and Beyond

The headland at Te Matarae a Manaoterangi belonged to Ngati Poataniwha. Their pa and village, Ngutuwera, were behind Rongohau. This was close to their summer fishing grounds, where they caught pioke and other fishy delicacies.

Many tribes came here to fish for pioke. A lure would be cast expertly into a school of pioke, which leapt to catch the bait. One at a time the pioke were heaved quickly aboard. The nicest ones were eaten fresh and the others were baked, hung to dry and stored for later.

In time the Kawerau came to control large areas of west coast beaches and the Waitakere forest. Beautiful waterfalls cascaded among the trees, and the huge cave at Te Ana areare near Tokatu was sometimes used for meetings or social gatherings. The Kawerau were a very proud tribe and they expected all visitors to respect them, even the highest rangatira. All the other

tribes knew that the Kawerau had great mana. Their history went back a long time. The Kawerau were very independent and did not rely on other people, but in the end this was their downfall, as constant raids fron Nga Puhi killed off most of the men.

Te Kawerau a Maki

Around the 1600s Maki married women from several tribes. Some were Kaipara women, while one of them, Rotu, was descended from the chief Te Murupaenga. She was a Ngati Whatua, so Maki also claimed to be a relative of the Tainui people.

The Nga Oho people had lived in the Waitakeres, mainly at Whatipu, since Maui pulled up Te Ika roa a Maui. Maki sent a taua to attack these people. At first there seemed to be no resistance, but at the entrance to the Pararaha Valley they were ambushed. Maki himself then arrived with more warriors, and at Wai-te-tura they conquered the Nga Oho.

Several Ngati Awa married Nga Oho women. Maki also married again, and his wife had a son whom he named Kawerau. From this boy the tribe at Waitakere was named Te Kawerau a Maki.

Chief Te Mana

In the time of the chief Te Mana, Kauri Point was called Te Matarae-a-Mana. Te Mana married Waikahuia, an important chieftainess from Maungakiekie. She was Kiwi Tamati's sister. This marriage meant Te Mana earned considerable respect with the Waiohua, but it also caused him a lot of worries he did not have before.

Kiwi Tamati would often visit Matarae during the shark-fishing season. Te Mana's problems began when Kiwi went on his visit to Kaipara. In the Maungakiekie story Kiwi murdered many of his hosts, as well as a group of Kaipara women who were gathering shellfish at Te Whau when his party were escaping back to Maungakiekie.

Te Mana was in an awkward position as he was married to Kiwi's sister. He managed to keep out of some trouble, however, and Te Matarae was one of the few pa that was not wrecked in the battles afterwards. Te Mana's other

villages were attacked by the Waiohua in the great battles at the Manukau. Ngati Whatua also attacked, and many chiefs were killed, including Kiwi Tamaki. Only the village of Te Matarae was spared. Te Mana managed to live out his natural life there, and died in peace in about 1790.

Tribal Kawerau women faced constant worry when their men went to war, not knowing if they would return home. Because many of the men were lost in battles the women and children took over many of their tasks. They had to be strong, otherwise there would be no Kawerau tribe. They relied on the forest for protection, disappearing into the bush when danger threatened. Most of the paths were single file to avoid the threat of ambush. The country was steep and rugged, so it was difficult for anyone to find the women and their children.

When times were peaceful they spread out along the Waitemata Harbour. In the places where they chose to settle for a while they would plant gardens and go fishing. In some places the clay soil made it too hard to garden with the ko. Instead they planted their kumara in the volcanic soil at Lake Pupuke and Takapuna.

The Kawerau did not stay for long at any one place, but they had a natural stronghold at Kauri Point. This pa had high cliffs, and ditches were dug on the inland sides. To get to the pa people had to cross a narrow, winding pathway, and a wooden stockade was also built here. Despite this the pa was not used very much.

Later Ngati Whatua, with help from the giant Kawharu, destroyed most of the Kawerau villages as utu for some unnecessary murders. They then retreated north, although in time they made peace with the Kawerau. Much later Kawharu went to visit his sister at Kaipara, and it was here that he was finally killed.

Waiheke

Oneroa

Onetangi

PATUKIRIKI

URI KARAKA

Maunganui

Putiki

Whakanewha

Rangihoua

Awaawaroa

Omaru

The Uri Karaka

The Uri Karaka were the first people to settle on Waiheke Island. They became famous because they made excellent nets and were very good fishermen. They made fragile rafts of woven flax stalks and raupo leaves, with sails made from the same materials. When they went to war, as they often did, they sailed fearlessly on these delicate craft. The often rough waters of Te Maraetai tossed the little mohiki about but it didn't worry them. When a war started they battled courageously with their kopero. Their only other claim to fame was that they introduced hue into Aotearoa and grew only these in their gardens. They fished and caught birds for their food.

Around the year AD 1150 the chief Toi-te-Huatahi, the Navigator, received sailing instructions from Kupe, an earlier explorer. At this time Toi was living in Tahiti. He travelled to Aotearoa and stopped in the Tamaki region to repair his canoe and to rest. Toi found there were many Maruiwi on Waiheke and they were not very friendly. Despite this some of his people decided to stay, but Toi sailed southwards.

Maeaea

Fifty years later the chief Maeaea accepted an invitation to a feast at Omaru near Awaawaroa on Waiheke. He arrived with a party of warriors who were descendants of Toi's. During the feast the hosts, the Uri Karaka, threw hand nets over them all and got them well tangled before using their tao to stab them all to death. This area is now known as Te Rore a Maeaea.

Maeaea's tribe set out to inflict a horrific utu on the Uri Karaka for these terrible murders. Their taua travelled hurriedly to attack at Waiheke. So successful were they that only a few Uri Karaka were left. Most of these were women, who were captured and taken as wives or slaves. Maeaea and his people now owned Waiheke.

Te Kauea, one of Toi's grandsons, was not at all happy about this revenge. He felt that it was not severe enough. Down in Whakatane, where most of Toi's relatives now lived, he gathered together a large taua. As they travelled up through the Waikato they massacred the tribal groups from the Waikato,

Hauraki and Kaipara whom they met on the way. After this rout they settled at Kaipara. Eventually Te Kauea and his son Tara-mai-nuku claimed ownership of the Hauraki foreshore and its islands, including Waiheke.

Marutuahu

About the year 1500 Hotunui and his wife lived in Kawhia. Hotunui was a descendant of the Tainui. When his wife was expecting a child Hotunui did a very foolish thing. He stole seed kumara from his brother-in-law's storehouse and fled from the village. He couldn't think of any other way to avoid being punished. Before he left he told his wife to call the baby Marutuahu if it was a boy. This was in memory of the garden that had been dug ready for the kumara planting.

Eventually Hotunui arrived at Hauraki and decided to settle there.

Some time passed after Marutuahu was born, and he grew into a fine young warrior. He decided to travel north in search of his father. He found Hotunui living at Wakatiwai, where the tribe treated him as a poor common person instead of the great chief he was. Marutuahu captured these people, who had not shown his father proper respect, and killed them all.

Marutuahu liked the Hauraki area so he decided to stay here. This included living at Waiheke Island. It wasn't long before he had great mana. He spent the rest of his life there, raising his family and ruling the people.

Some say Hotunui was falsely accused as his big feet obliterated the footprints of the real thief who was out and about that same night.

Raids and More Raids

Much later Tama-te Kapua beached the Arawa canoe on the seashore at Rangihoua, near Putiki, to rest and repair the rope lashings that had been damaged during the long sea voyage. One of the Maori women, Princess Kura, decided she liked the island and wanted to stay there, so several of those on the canoe went ashore with her. Kura and her friends settled at O a Kura, while Kumatamomoe, Tama's son, took ownership of the island by naming it Motu-nui-o-Kahu. Some of his family soon chose to settle on a cone-shaped hill inland from the sea. There a fort was built, and named Te Putiki-o-Kahu.

Taking possession of a chosen area was the ancient way of becoming the owner when no one else had claimed it. Because the Arawa people now had ownership of Waiheke those on the Tainui canoe travelled further on to other parts of the Waitemata and went ashore there.

Across the Hauraki Gulf the Arawa chief Tamatekapua and his people settled at Moehau. In time his grandson, Huarere, was born. Huarere grew up to be a strong and commanding person. He took over the control of the people who were the earlier owners of Moehau, and his tribe, Ngati Huarere, eventually owned all of the Hauraki Gulf and its islands.

The Ngati Huarere, and others living at Waiheke, set about strengthening their pa. This included Putiki o Kahu and Mt Maunganui. Some say the Waiohua copied the layouts used here for the fortifications of their mainland pa. In all, 39 pa sites have been found on Waiheke. Around 12 of these were in places that were very difficult to reach, and most warring parties could not easily attack them.

Several invasions took place in this area. Around AD 1450 the chief Maki, who was from Taranaki, set off with his Ngati Awa taua and conquered the Waikato, Tamaki and Kaipara. At Waiheke he besieged the Putiki pa and captured the defenders.

The second invasion took place in about 1680, when the Ngati Whatua chief Kawharu led a hostile taua to win the Tamaki isthmus from the Waiohua. Kawharu was a giant warrior who fearlessly fought all the way to Takapuna. Putiki pa was again besieged, but most of the inhabitants had already fled at the time of Maki's vicious attack. Kawharu made peace with these people but still returned home with the slaves and precious possessions he collected after each battle.

99

More trouble came when Kahurautao and other Hauraki chiefs were invited to visit the Waiohua at Maungawhau. The Ngati Huarere living at Putiki pa had become a subtribe of the Waiohua after making a pact by marriage with them. Back at Maungawhau, the chief Kahurautao and others were murdered by the Waiohua, which left the Waiheke people at risk of utu from Ngati Paoa.

The Hauraki Ngati Paoa tribes soon organised a large war party and again Putiki pa was besieged to settle the utu for these murders. Ngati Huarere suffered the blame for the murders because they were related to the Waiohua. Ngati Paoa completely destroyed this subtribe and became the new owners of Waiheke.

About Ngati Paoa

Way down at Taupiri, the Tainui chief Paoamana lived on the bank of the Waikato River. One day his brother Mahutu came visiting. Paoamana asked his wife Tauhakaru to cook food for them but she refused. They were short of supplies and she did not want her children to starve. Her refusal embarrassed Paoamana so much that he sulked then, to save face, he decided to leave and travel to Hauraki.

When he arrived at Piako he was greeted by Tukutuku, a chiefly woman and the great-granddaughter of Marutuahu. As she was not overly attractive she had been unable to find a suitable husband, but now Paoamana and Tukutuku married. It wasn't long before they had 10 children, all of whom were of chiefly standing. In time these people multiplied, and they came to own all the land from Piako to Hauraki, Tamaki and the islands in the Waitemata including Waiheke, and from Takapuna to Whangaparaoa.

Kapetawa

When Kapetawa, who was born on Waiheke, was a teenager he stayed with his sister Taurua at Kohimarama. She was the wife of the chief Taramokomoko. While Kapetawa was staying there he got into a lot of mischief and raided the kumara store of his brother-in-law. Taramokomoko was so angry that he took Kapetawa on a fishing trip and marooned him on Te Toka o Kapetawa (Bean Rock). The tide was coming in and Kapetawa was in danger of drowning.

He cried out pitifully. His sister saw the trouble he was in and rescued him, then she took him back to his tribe on Waiheke Island. Kapetawa never forgave Taramokomoko for this, and much later he decided to get his revenge.

When he became chief he led a surprise war party to attack Taramokomoko at Kohimarama and at Orakei, but his brother-in-law had fled to the North Shore. Kapetawa followed him, attacking and destroying all the villages he came across. He chased Taramokomoko along Waiwharariki (Takapuna Beach) to Maewao (Milford Beach) and all the way to Rahopara pa. During the battle there Kapetawa killed Taramokomoko, then he destroyed all the homes at the pa. He had satisfied his utu. After that no one lived at the pa so it rotted away.

While on the warpath Kapetawa also climbed the ridge between Rangihoua and Whakanewha. Here he left his 60 warriors and travelled to Te Putiki o Kahu alone in search of the refugees from Orakei. When he sneaked into the pa he found all the people in Mahiturua, the big house on the top of the hill. Everyone was talking about him. He ran into the house, and when the people recognised him he just as quickly escaped. As he left he pegged the sliding door shut and raced around jamming all the windows on the outside. Three sides of the house were made of raupo. Kapetawa set fire to this and burned everyone inside.

After Kapetawa had avenged Taramokomoko and sacked the Putiki pa he was satisfied and settled peacefully on Waiheke, never to go to war again.

Waitakere

The Beach and Forest

Some of the oldest volcanoes erupted in Waitakere between 6 and 22 million years ago. They rose five to six times higher than Ruapehu, Ngauruhoe and Tongariro. Two lines of volcanic action built the Scenic Drive and the west coast. Lion Rock fills the throat of one of these. Relentless winds, land slumping and heavy seas eroded and flattened these majestic mountains long before any humans existed.

At Muriwai there were toheroa in the sand. These became a local delicacy. The gannets nested at Otakamiro Point and at Oaia, and on the Motutara Islands. Sometimes fur seals rested at Oaia. The following stories are about this lovely area.

When Kupe first came to Aotearoa he travelled north along the Waitakere coastline. It wasn't long before he realised that his canoe was being followed, so he chanted a powerful karakia and cast his marowharu into the sea, leaving himself naked. This made the sea behind him too rough for those chasing him to continue the pursuit, and Kupe and his companions paddled on safely.

Te Toka Matua

Te Matua was a rock and she had two children who were also rocks. Just like all children they played happily on the beach and nearby. Their mother Te Matua warned them not to wander too far from her protection, but one of the children was often disobedient and wandered far off to play. This little rock became stuck far away from its mother, and is now called Te Tokapaoke. The well-behaved rock, which is called Te Tokapiri, is still close by Te Matua at Tahoro.

Tiriwa

Tiriwa was the most famous of the Turehu chiefs. The Turehu were fair-skinned folk who were able to perform superhuman feats. The Kawerau people did not think of them as fairies but others did.

Tiriwa and his folk ruled over the Waitakere Ranges from Karekare to Pararaha. He lived at the entrance to the lovely Pararaha valley, at O Tiriwa. Tiriwa was also capable of using magical powers. He could travel across the land in gigantic strides, leaving huge footprints as he stepped from one place to another. One of these imprints can be seen in the gully at the south end of Karekare Beach: Te Morere nui o Tiriwa, the great stride of Tiriwa.

Tiriwa also features in one of the stories about the creation of Rangitoto; see 'The Turehu Myth' on page 76.

The geological forms on the spectacular cliff at Mercer Bay are also said to have been made by Tiriwa.

Mokoroa

There is a creek in the Waitakeres called Mokoroa. A giant taniwha once lived there. Mokoroa had a fierce jaw, an extremely powerful tail, a spiny back and an enormous appetite. He was the pet of the iwi of this area. Because he helped his whanau, they made sure that Mokoroa never went hungry.

In time the people were killed by an enemy taua and Mokoroa had to look after himself. He ate all the eels and koura he could find in the stream, but he was always hungry. He began to snatch strangers from the forest trails, eating them gratefully.

Something had to be done to make the forest safe again, so Tai-oa-roa gathered his warriors together. They crept up to Mokoroa's sleeping pool in the creek and laid a gigantic net, then they hid in the bushes. When Mokoroa settled for the night they raced out and wrapped the net tightly around the taniwha. Mokoroa writhed and struggled violently and managed to kill several of his attackers, but eventually he became so tangled up in the net that there was no escape. Then Tai-oa-roa positioned himself carefully where he was able to raise his spear high enough to thrust it deeply into the taniwha's heart and kill him. Since that time all that has remained of the taniwha is his tail.

Parekura

In the Waitakere area was a lovely garden called Mara o Parekura which was very close to Anawhata. It was here in the summer that Parekura and her husband Panuku would come to stay, to plant and look after their kumara and gourd crops.

Nihotupu, one of the last Turehu people, lived deep in the forest at Te Wao nui a Tiriwa. One day he came to visit this garden, and took a basketful of hue. Parekura was busy checking how her plants were growing, and when Nihotupu saw her he instantly decided he liked her very much. So without any warning he captured her and dragged her off to his Rua o te whenua (cave in the land).

Parekura was very frightened but she thought quickly. As she was being dragged away she plucked toroa feathers from her cloak and dropped them on the path. She hoped that her rescuers would find her this way.

When Panuku realised that Parekura had disappeared he set off to look for her. When he saw the toroa feathers on the path he realised that only Parekura could have put the feathers of the seabird there, and he followed the trail.

It was not long before he found Nihotupu's Rua o te whenua. He acted quickly and was able to surprise Nihotupu and kill him. Much relieved, he was then able to rescue Parekura. After this the area became known as Te Awe ka tutu — 'the feather that summoned help'.

Erangi

Around 600 years ago there lived a young Maori maiden called Erangi. In time she met and fell in love with a handsome man from the inland pa at Puketotara. These two would often meet in secret, and in time Erangi gave birth to a cute little baby.

Erangi's family had found out about her secret lover, and because they disapproved of the match they forbade her to see him again. They kept a close watch on Erangi and the baby, and she was not allowed to travel very far from the seaside pa. This made Erangi desperate to leave, and she waited for her opportunity. There was only one way to escape. She would have to swim.

When no one was looking she tied her baby high on her shoulders and plunged into the sea. Unnoticed, she swam strongly northwards across the bay called Te Awa kau waha ia, which is now called Kauwahaia. The current was very strong, but Erangi did not give up. The water splashed around the baby's face but did not harm it. Eventually, some two kilometres up the coast, at Te Waharoa, Erangi and her baby came ashore. Erangi started to walk inland towards Puketotara pa, but after such an exhausting swim she needed to rest a while. She stopped by the Waioriori stream, and here she softly sang an oriori to soothe her baby. Her lover, who was snaring birds nearby, heard her singing. He was overjoyed to have found her again, and together they travelled to his pa where they lived happily for the rest of their days.

Hinerangi

A young chieftainess lived at Wai te tura. Her people were the Nga Oho, and they called her Hinerangi in honour of a famous Turehu ancestor. Hinerangi was truly very beautiful, very skilled and because of her ancestry many young rangatira came hoping to marry her. Hinerangi eventually fell in love with a young chief from Karekare and went to live in his village. They were extremely happy and could not be separated.

One day an unfortunate aitua happened. Close to where they lived at Tahoro was Te Kawa Rimurapa. This was a popular fishing place, and it was here that Hinerangi's husband and two of his friends went to fish. As is common in the Piha area huge waves often pounded the beaches, and on this day one swept the two friends off the reef into the sea. Although they could swim well they made no headway in the rough surf. Hinerangi's husband was distraught when he saw the trouble they were in. He dived into the foaming waters in an attempt to rescue his friends but, tragically, they were all swept out to sea and drowned.

Hinerangi was bereft and rushed to Te Ahua Point where she gazed tearfully out to sea, hoping to spot her husband. It was not to be. Hinerangi longed to get her husband back, so she sat grieving on the rocks at Te Ahua Point for days until her broken heart also killed her. Her spirit began the journey to Te Rerenga Wairua to find the spirit of her beloved husband. To this day her sad face can be seen on the rock face of the point where she sat, afterwards called Te Ahua o Hinerangi.

Glossary

ahua   shadow, shape, form

aitua   tragic accident

Akarana   Auckland

akiaki   red-billed gull

Aotea   the harbour near Kawhia

Arataki-haere   the path of single file

ariki   chief or lord

atahu   a ceremony to fan the flame of love

Awanui o Perehu   the channel of Perehu, the Rangitoto Channel

haka   war dance

hakena   coffin

hape   club foot

hapu   smaller groups related to iwi but living in separate villages

heitiki   a greenstone pendant

heru   comb

hinepuhi   set aside for an important marriage

hoeroa   a throwing weapon

hue   a gourd

Io   god

irirangi   voice, spirit

iwi   people

kahurangi   a jewel

karakia   prayer

Karangahape   area now called Cornwallis

karoro   black-backed gull

kaupapa   core matter or substance, plan, rule, topic

Kawharu   a giant chief of Ngati Whatua
kereru   wood pigeon
Koheraunui   the southwest hill at Three Kings
kopero   throwing spear
kopura   kumara, sweet potato
koto   Maori wooden spade
kotuku   white heron

Mahuika   goddess of fire
mana   power
manehau   a type of fern
mara   garden
Marama   the moon
marowharu   a kilt-like garment worn by chiefs
Marotiri   now called Cutter Rock
Mataaho   god of volcanoes
Maungakiekie   hill of the kiekie plant, One Tree Hill
Maungarei   the watchful mountain, now called Mt Wellington
Maungataketake   volcano now called Elletts Mountain
Maungauika   the mountain of Uika at North Head, Devonport
Maungawhau   hill of the whau tree, Mt Eden
mauri   mascot
mere   club
Moehau   now called Cape Colville
mohiki   raft or catamaran
Motuihe   correctly, Motuaihenga, 'Ihenga's Island'
Motukorea   now called Browns Island
Motutapu   Holy Island, named by Taiheku of the *Tainui* canoe

Nga Tau Mangere   the lazy winds, now called Mangere Mountain
Ngati Titahi   the people of Titahi
Ngutuwera   'burnt lips', a little bay west of Kauri Point
niti   dart
nui   big

ohaki   dying instruction

Omaru now Woodside Bay, Waiheke

Onemaewao Milford Beach, the fairies' beach

Onetangi murdering sands

Ora-waho the passageway between Rangitoto and Motutapu; these islands are now joined by a causeway

oriori lullaby

Oruawharu Islington Bay, between Rangitoto and Motutapu

Owairaka now called Mt Albert

Owhatihue the breaking of the gourd. This was a small pa near the southern base of Maungawhau

pahu gong

Pakuranga now called Pigeon Mountain

Pakuranga-rahihi refers to the battle of the sun's rays

Paruroa now called Muddy Creek, near Titirangi

patupaiarehe fairy people, the children of the mist

pere spear

pioke shark

Pitoitoi Riverhead

piupiu flax skirt

piwakawaka fantail

pukaea a two-metre-long trumpet

Puketapapa now called Mt Roskill

Puketutu the small island to the west of Mangere

Puponga at Cornwallis, the headland

puta gap

Putiki a pa site on Waiheke, also called Putiti

Putiki o Kahu the topknot of Kahu

Pututahi 'killed together'; a place near St John's College

rangatira chief

Rangi and Papa the sky father and the earth mother

Rangi o Taiheku day of Taiheku, referring to the day the *Tainui* became stuck on a sandbank

Rangitoto blood from the sky; 'toto' is the name given to the black volcanic rocks on the island

Rarotonga now called Mt Smart

rehia seaweed

Remu-wera burnt hem of a garment, now Mt Hobson

ringa-matauranga hand knowledge

riroriro grey warbler

Rongohau now Kendall Bay, Shark Bay

rua cave or hole

rua o te whenua cave in the land

Ruaumoko the god of earthquakes

ruru morepork

Tahoro now called Union Bay

taiaha spear-club; Maori mostly swung the club end at each other

Takapuna the rock with a spring at North Head

Takuranga Mt Victoria

Tamakimakaurau Tamaki of the many lovers

Tamatea-nui the sun

Tane god of the forest

tangata whenua local people

tao spear

tapua monster

tara sea swallow (white-fronted fern)

taua war party

tauranga waka the place where canoes are hauled up

Taurere now called Taylor's Hill

Te Ahua o Hinerangi the likeness of Hinerangi

Te Ana o Kahumauroa the cave between North Head and
Cheltenham Beach

Te Aratahuna 'the pathway on the sandbank', at Puketutu Island

Te Aratopuni the dogskin path

Te Haukapua now called Torpedo Bay, Devonport

Te Henga now called Bethells Beach

Te Ika roa a Maui the long fish of Maui

Te Kai o Mokoika the food of Mokoika

Te Kawa Rimurangi the reef of the bull kelp

Te Kirikiri probably the Waihou or Piako river

Te Kopuke now called St John's College Hill

Te-Kotu-arai-roa the long sheltering island, Waiheke

Te Kurae a Tura Devonport

Te Marae-tai the enclosed sea between Waiheke and the mainland

Te Matarae-a-Mana 'Mana's brow', the headland at Bayswater Point

Te One-rangaa 'the stirred up sands' on Puketutu Island

Te pa o Tahuhu the pa of Tahuhu at Mt Richmond

Te Puke o Wairaka the hill of Wairaka, now called Mt Albert

Te Putiki o Kahu the topknot of Kahumatamamoe

Te Rerenga-ora-iti the leap of survivors

Te Rerenga Wairua the journey of the spirits

Te Rore-a-Maeaea the snaring of Maeaea

Te Roturuoureia the comb of Ureia the taniwha, near Point Erin

Te Rua Maunga a mountain that stood where Lake Pupuke is now

Te Tatua a Riukiuta now called Three Kings

Te Tauoma on the western shore of the Tamaki River near Purchas Hill

Te Ti Tutahi the cabbage tree standing alone, near the main road at Newmarket

Te Toangaroa now called Mechanics Bay

Te Toka o Kapetawa the rock of Kapetawa, Bean Rock

Te Tokapiri the rock that clung to its parent

Te Tokapoake the rock that wandered

Te Tokaroa the long reef, Meola Reef

Te Totara i Ahua the totara stands alone

Te Tuahu o Hua Kaiwaka the sacred shrine of Hua Kaiwaka

Te Upoko o Mataaho the head of Mataaho, now called Mangere Mountain

Te Upu Pakore Newton Gully

Te Wao nui a Tiriwa the great forest of Tiriwa

tewhatewha a spear-axe; the blunt side was swung at the opponent and the axe head gave weight to the swing. The sharp point was for stabbing

tihi mountaintop

tipi   to cast glamour

tipua   devil, strange, foreign

Titirangi   the edge of the heavens, a veronica plant

toheroa   a shellfish delicacy

tohi   ceremony with sprinkling of water

tohunga   priest or witchdoctor

toroa   albatross feather

Tu   god of war

tuahu   shrine, sacred place

uhanga   a mourning ceremony

utu   revenge

waewae-kotuku   crane's foot; named after the way footrests were tied to ko

wahi tapu   sacred place

Waiheke   cascade waters

Wai-puhi-nui   the name of the battle at Puhinui

Waipuna   waters flowing from a spring

Wairoa   now called Clevedon

Waitakere   waters bubbling forth

Wai te tura   wide or expansive bay, now North Piha

Waiwharariki   Takapuna Beach

Wakatiwai   probably Wakatatere, a creek near Shoal Bay

wananga   ceremonial gatherings

wao   forest

whanau   family

whare   house